To
Drew
I help people win!

Ken Blanch
3/14

Thank you for buying this book.

It is our sincere hope that this book guides you, your people, and your organization to the highest levels of satisfaction and performance. Please join our www.LeaderChat.org community where you can interact with others who strive to help people win at work.

—Ken Blanchard and Garry Ridge

Helping People
Win at Work

Helping People Win at Work

A Business Philosophy Called "Don't Mark My Paper, Help Me Get an A"

Ken Blanchard
Garry Ridge

Vice President, Publisher: Tim Moore
Associate Publisher and Director of Marketing: Amy Neidlinger
Editorial Assistant: Pamela Boland
Operations Manager: Gina Kanouse
Digital Marketing Manager: Julie Phifer
Publicity Manager: Laura Czaja
Assistant Marketing Manager: Megan Colvin
Cover Designer: Chuti Prasertsith
Design Manager: Sandra Schroeder
Managing Editor: Kristy Hart
Project Editor: Lori Lyons
Copy Editor: Gayle Johnson
Proofreader: Apostrophe Editing Services
Indexer: Cheryl Lenser
Compositor: Nonie Ratcliff
Manufacturing Buyer: Dan Uhrig

FT Press offers excellent discounts on this book when ordered in quantity for bulk purchases or special sales. For more information, please contact U.S. Corporate and Government Sales, 1-800-382-3419, corpsales@pearsontechgroup.com. For sales outside the U.S., please contact International Sales at international@pearson.com.

Eighth Printing: October 2012

ISBN-10: 0-13-701171-7
ISBN-13: 978-0-13-701171-1

Pearson Education LTD.
Pearson Education Australia PTY, Limited.
Pearson Education Singapore, Pte. Ltd.
Pearson Education North Asia, Ltd.
Pearson Education Canada, Ltd.
Pearson Educación de Mexico, S.A. de C.V.
Pearson Education—Japan
Pearson Education Malaysia, Pte. Ltd.

Library of Congress Cataloging-in-Publication Data

Blanchard, Kenneth H.
  Helping people win at work: a business philosophy called, "don't mark my paper, help me get an a" : helping people win at work / Ken Blanchard, Garry Ridge.
    p. cm.
  ISBN 978-0-13-701171-1 (hardback : alk. paper) 1. Leadership. 2. Performance--Management. 3. Communication in organizations. I. Ridge, Garry, 1945- II. Title.
  HD57.7.B557 2009
  658.4'092--dc22
                              2009000598

To Ted and Dorothy Blanchard
who taught Ken that effective leadership
is not about position power
but about earning the trust and respect
of those you lead

To Bob and Jean Ridge
who taught Garry about character
and determination

and

To the tribe members of WD-40 Company
who have worked hard to put Garry's beliefs
into action

Contents

Introduction

KEN BLANCHARD

IN WINTER 2007, my colleagues and I from The Ken Blanchard Companies published *Leading at a Higher Level*. It pulled together the best thinking from more than twenty-five years of working together. It truly is *Blanchard on Leadership*. Our hope is that someday, everywhere, everyone will know someone who leads at a higher level.

When you lead at a higher level, the development of the people you're leading is just as important as the performance and results you desire. This is true whether you're leading students in class, youngsters on a team, parishioners at church, family members at home, or direct reports at the office.

In the business realm, the importance of developing people applies to both your employees and your customers. In short, the well-being and personal growth of the people you're leading are as important—if not more so—as the goals you seek to achieve.

As a result, we define leading at a higher level as the process of achieving worthwhile results while acting with respect, care, and fairness for the well-being of all involved.

THE LEADING AT A HIGHER LEVEL SERIES

The feedback on *Leading at a Higher Level* has been tremendous. Now that people know our curriculum, the only additions they have requested are in-depth examples of how leaders and their organizations have taken aspects of *Leading at a Higher Level* and put them into practice while maintaining a dual focus on performance and people. We decided to introduce the *Leading at a Higher Level* series to do just that.

I am thrilled that the first book in this series is with Garry Ridge, president and CEO of WD-40 Company. Conventional wisdom tells us that if it isn't broken, we shouldn't fix it. WD-40 Company wasn't broken when Garry stepped into the role of CEO in 1997. It was a brand leader that had produced consistent profits for more than forty years. WD-40's philosophy and culture were conservative, and that cautious approach had served the company well. Yet that wasn't good enough for Garry because he knew the company's best was yet to come.

Garry bucked tradition and messed with success. Among the many changes that he and his colleagues initiated was a performance review system that has elevated Partnering for Performance—a major aspect of *Leading at a Higher Level*—to whole new heights. This process has helped WD-40 Company to become a darling on Wall Street.

Since becoming CEO and implementing the "Don't Mark My Paper, Help Me Get an A" performance review system, Garry has seen the company's annual sales more than triple. They have grown from $100 million—with only 30 percent coming from domestic sales—to more than $339 million in 2008—with a more balanced 53 percent coming from sales outside the United States. During that time the company's capital value has nearly doubled, from $320 million to $600 million. And with sales per employee at $1.1 million, WD-40 Company is an extraordinarily efficient operation.

Remarkably, they have accomplished this financial feat while making WD-40 Company a great place to work. The 2008 WD-40 Company Employee Opinion Survey found an astonishing 94 percent of the company's people to be fully engaged in their work.

PARTNERING FOR PERFORMANCE

At its best, leadership is a partnership—one that involves mutual trust and respect between two people who work together to achieve common goals. When that occurs, both leader and direct report have an opportunity to influence each other. Both parties play a role in determining how things get done. In other words, it's all about *we*, not me.

My thinking on this dates back to my ten-year experience as a college professor, when I was periodically in trouble with the faculty. What drove them crazy more than anything was that at the beginning of every course I often gave my students the final exam. When the faculty found out about that, they asked, "What are you doing?"

I said, "I thought we were supposed to teach these students."

The faculty said, "We are, but don't give them the final exam ahead of time!"

I said, "Not only will I give them the final exam ahead of time, what do you think I'll do throughout the semester? I'll teach them the answers so that when they get to the final exam, they'll get As. You see, I think life is all about helping people get As—and not force-fitting them into a normal distribution curve."

Yet many organizations do exactly that. They force their managers to evaluate, judge, and sort out their people according to that wonderful mathematical formula. A woman came up to me recently almost in tears. She said, "I wish I had eight people reporting to me."

I asked, "Why?"

She said, "Because I have two outstanding people. With seven people I can rate only one of them high, but with eight, I could recognize both."

Other companies do even worse than the normal distribution curve, and force their managers to rank-order their people. In both cases, the worst-case scenario you can have as a manager is to have a group of high performers working for you. How do you sort them out? What a sad state of affairs.

In most organizations managers are expected to rate only a few people high, a few people low, and the rest as average performers. Even when a company doesn't have a normal distribution curve evaluation system, managers are afraid to rate all their people high, because then the managers would be rated low. They would be accused of being "too easy" or "soft" managers. As a result, the normal distribution curve is alive and well throughout the world.

The absurdity of that reality comes through when I ask managers, "How many of you go out and hire losers so that you can fill the low slots?" Everyone laughs, because they know they hire either winners—people who already have a good track record in what they are being hired to do—or potential winners—people who they think can become winners with the proper supervision and coaching. They don't hire losers. Then why do a certain number of people have to lose—by getting rated low?

I don't think they do. That's why I often handed out the final exam at the beginning of the semester. Was that exam easy? No way. I didn't give true/false or multiple-choice tests. My exams were tough. But the goal I had throughout the semester was to partner with my students by teaching them how to answer those tough questions. I wanted my students to win—and so did they. We were partners in helping them get an A.

After learning about this philosophy, Garry Ridge implemented "Don't Mark My Paper, Help Me Get an A" as a major theme at WD-40 Company. Why? Because it is so consistent with his leadership point of view—his beliefs about leading and motivating people. He is so emphatic about this concept that he would fire a poor performer's manager rather than the poor performer if he found out that the manager had done nothing to help that person get an A.

There aren't enough leaders like Garry Ridge. His story is the ultimate real-world example of what leading at a higher level in the area of Partnering for Performance looks like, and I'm excited about sharing it with you.

GARRY RIDGE

At the age of forty I decided it was time to expand my learning. Although I had long ago earned a diploma from Sydney Technical College and was serving as CEO of WD-40 Company, I wanted to confirm what I thought I knew and learn what I didn't. So I enrolled in the Master of Science in Executive Leadership degree program at the University of San Diego. That's where I met Ken Blanchard and heard him talk about his "give them the final exam at the beginning of the semester" philosophy. That degree program has become the most influential learning experience in my life so far. I was not asked to go to the library to expand on what I had learned in class, but rather to take my learnings back to my company to test their application in the real world. That's when I became excited about implementing Ken's "final exam" philosophy at WD-40 Company.

It's been a joy for me to work with Ken on this book, which shares our WD-40 performance review philosophy. In reading it, our story might be an alarm bell for you and the other leaders in your organization. Why do I say "alarm bell"? Let me tell you a personal story that will answer that question.

In late July 2007 I was near the end of a twenty-six-day, round-the-world business trip. I had gone from San Diego to Sydney and Perth, Australia, and then to Shanghai, and finally to London.

After a ten-hour flight I landed at Heathrow around four o'clock and made my way to my hotel in Mayfair. After a quick freshen-up, I was off for dinner with some members of the European leadership team. It had been a long day by the time I got back to the hotel around eleven that night.

Morning seemed to arrive doubly fast, especially since I had a full day of meetings ahead of me. Later, as I headed back to my hotel around four-thirty, I was looking forward to a relaxing night in London.

I bought a couple of beers at the store across from the hotel, got some takeout for dinner, and went to my room. I was ready to kick back, watch a little British comedy, and chill out for the night.

I got into my shorts and T-shirt and settled in for the night, warm and comfortable.

That was when the fire alarm sounded. Having stayed in lots of hotels, I had heard many alarms. I did what I usually do—ignored it. My life experience up to that point had been that in a matter of minutes the alarm would be turned off, management would apologize over the loudspeaker, and life would go on.

But that night the alarm continued to sound, and I was getting annoyed. This irritating alarm was interfering with my preplanned beer and British comedy!

It was the banging on the door that really got my attention. A security guard was making the rounds to be sure that the hotel was evacuated. At his insistence, I grabbed my cell phone and passport. Wearing just shorts, T-shirt, and those undersized slippers you get in the hotel, I headed down the six flights of stairs to the ground floor.

I had forgotten that it was winter in London. By the time I hit the street, I was reminded that shorts, T-shirt, and slippers were not the best attire at seven-thirty at night in the streets of Mayfair.

Police and sniffer dogs were everywhere. We were directed down the street and instructed to wait in an open park space in Berkley Square. So much for my warm room, beer, and British comedy!

About an hour went by. It started to rain. I was cold and getting wet. I certainly wasn't appropriately dressed. It was nearly nine o'clock when the all clear was given. There had been a bomb scare from someone leaving a backpack in the hotel lobby. Being on high alert, London takes such things seriously. Cold, wet, and unhappy, I returned to my room and headed straight for a hot shower to unfreeze.

Two days later I boarded a flight back to San Diego. As the plane took off, I began to reflect on my trip. My thoughts quickly went to my cold shutout from the bomb scare. It got me thinking how stupid I'd been to ignore the initial alarm. If I'd paid attention to that first alarm, I would have had time to dress more appropriately for the hours I was to spend in the winter rain of London. I could have done a lot better than shorts, T-shirt, and hotel slippers.

I realized that alarm bells have a purpose, especially if we choose to hear them and act on them. *Was there a Learning Moment here?* I wondered.

I started to think about how many alarm bells were going off in my life, personally and professionally, that I was choosing to ignore or that were being drowned out by the music and noise of life.

I took a piece of paper and made two columns: "personal" and "professional." I started to list all the alarm bells or warning sounds I could think of, and there were many. I'm twenty pounds overweight and don't get enough exercise. What if that's ruining my health? I don't tell my loved ones that I love them often enough. What if I'm losing their affection? I've been told I don't listen enough. What if I'm missing good feedback? WD-40 is an oil-based product—what if oil goes to $100 a barrel? What if, what if, what if!

By the time I finished, I had a full page. Now I could validate the impact of the alarm bell and make a choice. I could hear it and react to it, or I could ignore it. Would ignoring it put me out in the cold?

The concept of alarm bells has been a real aha for me—a wonderful Learning Moment. I realize now that we often let past experience rule our current behavior. It's also easy to let the music of life drown out alarm bells. Sometimes good and bad sounds block our awareness, especially when things are going well. The cheering of success sometimes blinds us, and we miss the real opportunities that can come from success.

Since that trip I have shared my alarm bell learnings with many, and the impact has been amazing. It's a simple exercise of forced awareness that helps us focus on what matters so that we can make conscious choices.

Now back to you. Could you be ignoring an alarm bell about your performance review system? A few minutes of brutal honesty could go a long way toward uncovering any buried alarm bells in this area. Ask yourself:

- How do your people respond to your performance review system?

- Do they think it's fair?

- Do they get feedback at the end of the year that they never received throughout the year?

- Does your system build trust and respect between your managers and their people?

I hope reading about our WD-40 Company "Don't Mark My Paper, Help Me Get an A" philosophy will be an alarm bell for top managers and human resources development people about their performance review system. As I travel around the world, I still see too many performance review systems where some people *have* to lose. If you have that kind of system and think it's good, I wonder what other alarm bells you might be avoiding.

HOW THIS BOOK IS ORGANIZED

This book is divided into four parts. In Part One, Garry reveals the fundamentals of WD-40 Company's "Don't Mark My Paper, Help Me Get an A" performance review system. Parts Two and Three will help you understand that effective change—the kind of change Garry and the folks at WD-40 Company have achieved with their performance review system—is more about managing the journey than announcing the destination.

In Part Two you will read about the cultural changes that had to be made in how things were done at WD-40 Company before the performance review system could be revamped.

In Part Three Garry shares his leadership point of view—what he expects of people and what they can expect of him—and where those beliefs about leading and motivating people came from. If a change effort is not central to the top managers' thinking, it probably won't succeed, since top management's support is so key to the effective implementation of any change.

In Part Four Ken shares the "Simple Truths" that he and his colleagues have learned over the years. They help explain why Partnering for Performance, as practiced at WD-40 Company, works—and how it can work for you.

The big-picture question for you as you read this book is:

**Are you partnering for performance
with your people,
or is your performance review system
an alarm bell?**

Read on!

ONE

Don't Mark My Paper, Help Me Get an A

GARRY RIDGE

AS I SHARE with you how we successfully implemented our "Don't Mark My Paper, Help Me Get an A" philosophy into our performance review system, we'll cover three aspects of an effective performance review system: *planning, execution,* and *review and learning.* These set the context around which everything in our new performance review system was done. During this discussion you will notice that when I talk about our managers, I refer to them as "tribal leaders" and the people who report to them as "tribe members."

To shift people's mind-set about learning and to set up our "Don't Mark My Paper, Help Me Get an A" philosophy, I asked our people to think of us not as a "team" but rather as a "tribe." Using tribal terminology gave me a vehicle to talk about a wide range of organizational attributes that were important to WD-40 Company, rather than just the attributes I'd be limited to if I were to use the word "team." A team is about winning and getting stuff done in a positive way. While that's important, a tribe is a much richer concept.

A tribe is a place you belong; a team is something you play on once in a while.

The tribal concept set the tone for the open communication we needed in our company. It also helped establish a partnership philosophy that is necessary to implement the "Don't Mark My Paper, Help Me Get an A" concept. I'll talk about this in more depth in Part Two, "Building the Right Culture."

PLANNING

When it comes to planning, once a year every tribal leader has a conversation with each of his or her direct reports to establish the tribe member's final exam. A final exam has three parts: essential functions, SMART goals, and values.

The whole "Don't Mark My Paper, Help Me Get an A" process starts with an agreement on essential functions. Essential functions primarily describe the responsibilities of tribe members within their unique job position. For example, a salesperson's essential functions could include sales, administration, customer service, team contribution, and account management.

Before we start our "Don't Mark My Paper, Help Me Get an A" process at the beginning of the year, we e-mail everyone in the company—including new and promoted people—a description of their essential functions with a comment that says, "This is the current essential functions description we have on your position. Is this still the way you understand your job?" We give people their essential functions before agreeing on their final exam because we realize that tribe members know better than anybody else whether their jobs have changed. The discussion can explore whether a tribe member is overloaded and whether he or she needs to give up or redefine certain aspects of the job. Perhaps the tribe member needs to engage in additional training to develop more competencies. The essential functions description is a work-in-process document throughout the year.

The discussion with a new hire or promoted person obviously is a bit different. Our concern there is focused on "Is this the job you thought you accepted?"

Once tribe members are clear on their essential functions, three to five short-term SMART goals become their priority for their final exams. SMART is a widely used acronym for what a well-defined goal looks like:

- **S** stands for specific. It doesn't do much good to say to somebody, "I want you to improve in this area." That is not specific enough. Specific means it is observable and measurable. If you can't measure something, you can't manage it.

- **M** stands for motivational. Part of the alignment process involves getting clarity about whether this is a goal that the tribe member is excited about and willing to pursue. In analyzing anybody's performance potential, you have to look at both competence and commitment.

- **A** stands for attainable. You don't want to set a goal that is so hard that the person doesn't have a chance to achieve it. What you want are "stretch" goals. These are goals that are moderately difficult but achievable for the person. An A for one person may be quite different than an A for another person doing a similar job. Competence and experience have to come into play here.

- **R** stands for relevant. We believe in the 80/20 Rule: Eighty percent of what you want your people to accomplish comes from 20 percent of the activities they could focus on. Therefore, the three to five goals chosen for an individual should be ones that are most relevant to that job. In essence, this means that each goal chosen should directly contribute to the company's bottom line or support the efforts of those who do. For example, in accounting, a SMART goal could be set on promptness of payments for accounts receivable. A human resources SMART goal could be focused on retention and absenteeism. A SMART goal for marketing could be increasing the profit contribution of a brand or supporting the efforts of the salespeople. A SMART goal in the supply chain area might be focused on cost reduction.

- **T stands for trackable.** You don't want a goal that leaves you in the dark about how you'll get there, or that makes it hard to know how well somebody is doing on the goal until it's finished. You want a goal that you can track over time. That way, during periodic review sessions you can praise progress or redirect efforts, depending on how the individual is doing on the goal at that moment. You don't want to wait to praise or redirect somebody after the fact.

One of the things I've learned over the years is that:

All good performance starts with clear goals.

When establishing a final exam with someone, it's important to be certain that the person knows exactly what he or she is being asked to do. That's what establishing SMART goals does. It makes sure that people are being evaluated on observable, measurable goals, not on fuzzy, subjective expectations.

We take all this time to agree on essential functions and goals because, as Stephen Covey says, "Nearly all conflict comes from differences in expectations."

The rules at WD-40 Company are simple: If people attain their observable, measurable goals at the end of the fiscal year, they will get an A—as long as they're in good shape with the third part of the final exam—living the company values. I'll talk about our company values in Part Two, "Building the Right Culture." At WD-40 Company we don't just want good performers; we want good performers who are also good citizens—people who live our values. This means that a high performer who continually violates our values might be facing a career crisis.

EXECUTION

Once people are clear on their final exam and the observable, measurable goals that the exam consists of, we move on to execution. At this stage, people must begin to perform on their agreed-upon goals. This is where day-to-day coaching comes into play. This is a major emphasis in the "Don't Mark My Paper, Help Me Get an A" philosophy. In most organizations, as Ken suggested in the introduction, after goals are set, managers file them and don't think much about their people's performance until they realize they have to do their annual performance reviews. The only other time they think about their people's performance is when something goes wrong that is evident to everyone. These managers tend to manage by exception. When a red flag goes up, they go to work and start managing.

At WD-40 Company, agreeing on the final exam with a tribe member at the beginning of the fiscal year only begins the process. Now comes the key step:

The leader has to keep up his or her end of the partnership relationship on a day-to-day basis, helping and coaching the tribe member to get an A.

One of the concepts that helps drive day-to-day coaching at WD-40 Company is Situational Leadership® II, another important Blanchard concept I learned during the MSEL program at the University of San Diego. What attracted me to Situational Leadership® II is that its purpose is to increase the quality and quantity of conversations between leaders and their people. Ken will describe this concept in more detail in Part Four, "The Simple Truths about Helping People Win at Work," but let me share with you its essence.

According to Situational Leadership® II, there is no one best leadership style. It all depends on an individual's competence and commitment in a particular goal area. Competence depends on a person's knowledge and transferable skills from past experience, and commitment depends on a person's motivation and confidence. Competence has to do with skill, and commitment has to do with attitude.

Situational Leadership® II identifies four development levels people go through as they move from dependence to independence in doing a task. It's important to note that no individual is at any one stage in all the tasks that he or she is asked to perform. So when a tribe leader agrees with a tribe member on a final exam that includes three to five goals, the first step for both of them is to analyze that tribe member's development level on that particular goal. They ask, "Is the tribe member new and inexperienced on this task, or a skilled veteran? Is the tribe member excited and confident about doing the task?"

Why ask those questions? Because they will determine what leadership style is necessary for that particular goal. Does the tribe member, because of inexperience, need direction and support, or is she competent and committed enough to direct and support her own efforts? In other words, when it is necessary to increase tribe members' competence in particular goal areas, they need direction and supervision from their leaders. If tribe members need to build their commitment, they need support, encouragement, and involvement from their tribe leaders.

After a final exam is created, the process goes like this: leaders and tribe members together analyze the development level of the tribe member on each of his or her goals and determine the leadership style that is a match. Then they have to agree on a follow-up plan to implement an agreed-upon style. As the tribe member continues to develop, that style should change. What Situational Leadership® II does beautifully is assist people in determining what kind of help they need from their managers as they move toward their A in each of their agreed-upon goal areas. It provides the basis for the day-to-day coaching of tribe members.

REVIEW AND LEARNING

Continually planning and executing without the value of review and learning could blindside you with what we call a typhoon—a destructive event. That's when somebody makes a mistake that hurts both the organization and that person's reputation. Since we don't want that to happen, it is important to take time to pause, review progress, and look for any learning— whether or not a mistake has been made.

Pausing to learn often isn't part of business culture. A typical strategy is "Plan your work and work your plan." But that focuses all the energy on planning and execution. When people spend too much time planning and executing, it's all about operations, operations, operations. This doesn't allow time for people to figure out what's working and what isn't. An important thing to remember about execution is this: Don't get caught there. I would love for people to have a sign on their desk that says, "Don't just do something—sit there!" At WD-40 Company, we want to make sure we take time to find the learning in every action. That requires consistently reviewing what we're doing.

When it comes to reviewing, we ask these questions:

- What did we set out to do?

- What actually happened?

- Why did this happen?

- What will we do next time?

- What should we continue to do?

- What should we do differently?

At WD-40 Company the review and learning process is a continuous conversation throughout the year. Why do we say review and learning is an ongoing process? Because:

You don't want to save up feedback until somebody fails.

Periodically, you want to be able to give people feedback that either is positive or redirects their efforts.

To make feedback effective, **caring and candor** are important. *Caring* is behavior that demonstrates your concern about the person's development, professionally and personally. *Candor* permits a manager to deliver impactful feedback. That means being candid and honest with a person in a caring way. Candor and caring go hand in hand. With caring, you get to make deposits in your emotional bank account with a person.

Why is that important? Because sometimes you have to make withdrawals. No matter how caringly you give negative feedback, sometimes it hurts. And if you don't have the deposits when you make the withdrawals, you're in an awful place. But if the person you're dealing with knows you want him or her to succeed, the pain is short-lived and turns into a Learning Moment. At WD-40 Company, having Learning Moments is something we've worked hard to imbed in our culture.

Quarterly Informal/Formal Discussions

Four times a year all our tribe leaders have a conversation with each of our tribe members, which we call "informal/formal discussions." The first item of business is to review the agreed-upon final exam. Is it still relevant? In a lot of companies, after goals are agreed on at the beginning of the year, they are filed and seldom reviewed. Yet throughout the year different demands occur, and people are asked to do things that were not part of their original goals—or in our terms, "final exam." As a result, people are often evaluated at the end of the year on established goals that are no longer relevant. That's why each quarter our tribe leaders and tribe members review the final exam and make appropriate changes, if needed. If new goals are added, it is legitimate to take some old ones off the final exam.

After reviewing the final exam, the tribe leader and member begin to look at the tribe member's performance. In most organizations, at the end of the year every manager has to complete an evaluation of each of his or her people. It often is an agonizing and time-consuming process. The direct reports wait anxiously to see how they did—how their manager evaluated their performance. This gets particularly sticky when companies have a normal distribution curve, where managers are forced to sort out their people into a few winners, a few losers, and a lot of average performers. Even worse is when they have to rank-order their people from first to last.

At WD-40 Company, everybody has to complete only one performance evaluation—their own—and they do it every quarter for our informal/formal discussions. This evaluation is based on the final exam they agreed on at the beginning of the fiscal year. I don't fill out people's evaluations, nor do any of our tribe leaders. What we do is have a conversation one-on-one during our quarterly meeting and review each person's assessment of him- or herself. If a tribe leader disagrees on a tribe member's assessment, that's where caring and candor come to the forefront. It's not about sticking your finger in the tribe member's face and saying, "Hey, when you and I agreed on your final exam at the beginning of the year, you were going to do this. And right now we're not there." Rather, when we find a discrepancy between what was agreed upon and what's happening, we always ask, "What's going on in your life and your business that's not allowing what we expected to happen? How can I help?"

The other two key aspects of implementing our "Don't Mark My Paper, Help Me Get an A" philosophy are *accountability* and *responsibility*. Accountability means taking time to review progress and add value to the tribe member's mission to get an A. So accountability goes both ways—from the leader as well as the tribe member. Accountability is the opposite of entitlement. A lot of people want entitlement.

Entitlement means "You owe me."
Accountability means "We owe each other
for something we've agreed upon."

When we talk about responsibility, we're talking about addressing your and your tribe members' commitment to achieving an A. No finger-pointing is tolerated. It's a partnership. Both sides are responsible for the outcome. We don't play the blame game, because we know we are accountable and responsible, too. I firmly believe that reasonable people who absorb the same information and share the same values will probably arrive at the same point of view. If they don't, the differences can be worked out.

To take the fear out of these quarterly conversations, I tell people that not everyone has to get an A on every goal. In fact, a B is the best thing you can get in one of our informal/formal discussions, because a B says "I need help on this goal." I tell my people, "If you gave yourself a B somewhere in your quarterly review, you've got to know I'm on your side. Because I know you got a B and I want to be there next to you." Getting a B means "I can be better." It doesn't mean "I failed." Since I get to see everyone's review, our tribe members know that if they get a B on some part of their quarterly review, I'll come alongside their tribal leader and chat with him or her to see if there's any way I can help.

For example, I'm leaving for Europe this week, and I have a list of all the B people. Before I talk to tribe leaders about their tribe members' As, the first thing I'll do is talk to them about any Bs their people got. I'll say, "Hey, Fred, loved seeing your people's reviews. I see some of them got a few Bs. How can I help? What do we need to do to turn those Bs into As? Remember, our responsibility is all about helping people get As on their goals. If they aren't getting As, we've failed."

Can anybody get higher than an A on a goal? Yes, they can get an A+ on a goal if they've done the following:

- Consistently exhibited a high skill level

- Gone above and beyond to demonstrate our corporate values

- Taught others how to demonstrate corporate values

- Are a role model to others on that goal and can pass the test of public opinion—meaning that their reputation, exceptional contributions, and results in that area are well known by others

If tribe members don't get As or Bs at their quarterly informal/formal discussions, the next thing they can get is an L on a goal. What does that mean? It means those tribe members are in a learning mode on that goal. It's a new responsibility, and they need more time to gain competence. While they do not meet expectations on that goal, they are progressing to an acceptable level of competence.

Can tribe members get a C, D, or F on a goal at a quarterly informal/formal discussion? They can get a C, but no grade is lower than that. Getting a C on a goal means there has been a lack of effort, and tribe members need to apply themselves more consistently to meet expectations on that goal. An improvement plan should be in effect, and effort is necessary. A C also can indicate that little effort has been made to demonstrate corporate values while working on that goal, and the tribe member needs to demonstrate those values more frequently in that area.

This evaluation process is repeated at the end of every quarter as well as at the end of the year during the final annual review. It is important to reiterate that tribe leaders fill out a performance evaluation only on themselves. They do not fill out evaluation forms on the tribe members who report to them.

The evaluation form that tribe members fill out on themselves is a working document. (See Appendix A, "The WD-40 Company Goal Review Form.") The same form is used throughout the year. For example, when tribe members assess their performance for the second-quarter informal/formal discussion, that form also displays their first-quarter assessment. By the time their final self-assessment is completed at the end of the year, the form is completely filled out and includes an overall rating. It's just like when you were in school. You got graded separately for each course and got a grade point average at the end of the year.

In addition to a grade for each goal area, tribe members must evaluate themselves on whether they have demonstrated or visited each of the six corporate values. Each quarter and again at the end of the year, tribe members give examples of demonstrating each value. Remember, we are looking for tribe members who are both high performers *and* values-driven players.

Suppose at the end of the year a tribe member can't even maintain a B average. Now it's career planning time. If the manager has done everything possible to help that person get an A, including appropriately applying Situational Leadership® II, tribe member and tribe leader must sit down and decide what to do. The tribe member is obviously in the wrong position. If he or she is a values-driven tribe member, we may look for another position within WD-40 Company.

If the person is not a values-driven tribe member, and we think termination is necessary, we use a bit softer phrase than Donald Trump's "You're fired!" We just kindly say to someone, "If our culture of candor, caring, accountability, and responsibility doesn't work for you, let's share you with a competitor." WD-40 Company is not for everyone.

That said, WD-40 Company goes to great lengths to see that people are treated with dignity and respect. When someone is asked to leave our company, it is after a great deal of effort to keep that person. When people leave WD-40 Company, most of the time they feel treated with respect and do not harbor ill will for the company. That's the highest level of achievement in any company—to have people shake your hand as they leave involuntarily.

Suppose a manager came to me and said a person should be shared with the competition for a values problem, a performance problem, or both. I would ask, "What have you done to help that person get an A?"

> *If there isn't clear evidence that a plan was in place to help the tribe member get an A ... I would need to question that leader's commitment.*

In the final analysis, perhaps the manager is the one who needs to be shared with the competition.

You don't have to share a tribe leader with the competition more than once to get the attention of all the leaders and help them recognize that managing people is a partnership, not a purely judgmental role. We want as many of our people to win as possible.

MANAGING THE JOURNEY

One key factor that makes a change effort successful is follow-up. Without a learning environment, a clear vision, and rank-ordered values, it's hard to keep people on track. These, combined with our tribal culture, set the context that helped make our new performance review system successful.

TWO

Building the Right Culture

GARRY RIDGE

TO MAKE A SIGNIFICANT change in something as important as an organization's performance review system, you first have to focus on the culture. Culture refers to the assumptions, beliefs, values, customs, and behaviors of the organization's employees, supervisors, and leaders. In other words, culture is "the way we do things around here."[1] Impacting the WD-40 Company culture I inherited was not a quick fix. It required several steps before I could revamp our performance review system.

CREATING A LEARNING ENVIRONMENT

The first thing I tackled was breaking up the knowledge silos that were core to the old WD-40 Company culture. Why? I had been with WD-40 Company for almost ten years in international marketing before being named CEO. Coming from inside the company had its advantages. Being familiar with the existing culture, I knew where the trouble spots were.

At the time I stepped into my leadership role at the company, knowledge was the currency of the kingdom. Those who knew the most about how things worked guarded that knowledge—consciously or unconsciously—knowing that it gave them power. This led to a lot of silos of knowledge, which hurt us, because it hid what was working and what wasn't. I knew that breaking up these knowledge silos into what I called "fields of learning" would be the first step in creating a culture where learning was valued and shared, and information could move easily.

What keeps people in organizations from wanting to learn? They look at mistakes as career-damaging events rather than opportunities to learn. Therefore, they cover up mistakes in the hope that no one finds out.

What I needed to do was to help people realize that mistakes were inevitable but not necessarily fatal. To do that, I had to redefine the concept of "mistakes." I needed to teach people not to be afraid to fail. I had to earn their trust by showing that neither I nor any of our managers would take adverse action if someone tried something new and didn't succeed.

At WD-40 Company, when things go wrong, we don't call them "mistakes"; we call them "Learning Moments."

At these times, tribe members and their leaders look at missteps as learning opportunities. They applaud the chance to learn and grow and incorporate new knowledge into their work. This became key in our "Don't Mark My Paper, Help Me Get an A" process. In fact, this is how we get better all the time.

CLARIFYING OUR VISION AND VALUES

The second thing I tackled was clarifying the company's vision and values. A vision gives you a sense of direction, and values give you a compass to keep you on course. Having a clear vision and values is just as important as having a learning culture.

Vision

To me a clear vision must be more than a business case statement.

> *A clear vision must answer the question*
> *"What mountain do we want to climb?"*

A clear vision must be something that inspires people to do their personal best right now.

Our WD-40 vision is clear: We're in the squeak, smell, and dirt business. Our products fix squeaks and get rid of smells and dirt. In essence, we are in the quality-of-life business. By fixing squeaks and getting rid of smells and dirt in an almost magical way, we make people's lives better and, in the process, create positive, lasting memories for our customers.

I often tell the story of Nancy, who works in our mail room. One day as I was leaving the mail room, Nancy, who's worked there for years, was complaining about the WD-40 supplies she was packing up to go to our new China facility.

The next week I traveled to China to visit that new facility. As I looked out the window I saw a bunch of kids walking to school wearing these lovely uniforms and shoes. And I thought, "I'm sure WD-40 bought some of those shoes, because we employ about forty or fifty people here."

So I went back to Nancy and said, "Hey, Nancy, if you thought the effort you spent getting WD-40 materials ready to send to China was creating employment there—and, therefore, helping to put a pair of shoes on the feet of a little Chinese girl who now has the opportunity to learn and make a difference in the world—would that mean anything to you?"

She said, "Oh, absolutely."

I told her that's what had happened. Her whole attitude changed. What a memory-maker that was for her.

One of the ways we promote fun, lasting memories is to celebrate the creative uses of our products. In fact, our company has a rich folklore around the unique and sometimes just plain weird uses people have found for WD-40. For example, a bus driver in Asia once used WD-40 to remove a python that had coiled itself around the undercarriage of his bus. Another time police officers used WD-40 to remove a naked burglar who was stuck in an air conditioning vent. So in many ways we are in the quality-of-life and making positive, lasting memories business.

Values

Once the vision is set, values are needed as principles that guide our behavior while we're scaling the mountain we set out to climb. Values need to be simple yet strong, and they need to be clearly communicated as the only acceptable behavior. The rank-ordered values that guide our behavior at WD-40 Company are:

1. Doing the right thing
2. Creating positive, lasting memories in all our relationships
3. Making it better than it is today
4. Succeeding as a team while excelling as individuals
5. Owning it and passionately acting on it
6. Sustaining the WD-40 economy

Why is it important for our values to be rank-ordered? Because:

Life is about value conflicts. That means sometimes you can't honor two values at the same time.

For example, I often tell a story about my daughter, who used to have a job playing Mickey Mouse at Disneyland. I asked her, "What's your number-one value?" Everyone assumes it's having fun. It's not. The number-one value at Disney is safety. When Kate was in character as Mickey Mouse, if she was entertaining little Johnny, and little Susie fell over, Kate didn't have to think twice. She went to help Susie, even if Johnny cried.

Given the fact that *doing the right thing* at WD-40 Company is our number-one value, it is unacceptable to create a positive, lasting memory for a customer if what you're doing is illegal or unethical. *Doing the right thing* always trumps creating memories. How do people know what is the right thing to do? We think people intuitively know what's right. Haven't you heard little kids say, "That's not fair!" Who told them that? No one. They just know. At WD-40 Company we hire good people and expect them to do the right thing.

Another interesting thing to note in our values is our last value, *sustaining the WD-40 economy*. I've seen a number of companies that never mention financial well-being as a value. When you don't do that, everyone knows that the values are a joke. Why? Because when finances aren't going well, a lot of energy gets focused in that direction.

Ranking our financial value last among our other values tells people it's important—it's one of our core values—but we will do nothing to make money that compromises any of the other values. Stating the value as sustaining the WD-40 economy is broader than valuing profits. When people see the word "profit" they think, "All they care about is making money." When we talk about a thriving economy, it implies the well-being of all involved, not just top management.

A value is an underlying reason for how we choose to act and how we make decisions. A value is the "why" behind the "how to." These are not just words in a book somewhere—we actually try to determine how well we're living up to these values in our review system. At WD-40 Company, you either demonstrate or visit a value.

For example, caring is an important aspect of *creating positive, lasting memories in all our relationships*. Alec demonstrates this value if everyone who works with him says that he's always friendly and respectful to his colleagues throughout the company. This means that when he walks in the back door every day, he's just as friendly and respectful to the people in the mail room as he is to those in the executive suite.

Let's suppose that Bruce is nice to two people in the organization, because he knows they can help him accomplish what he wants. But when he walks in the back door every day, he treats the people in the mail room and warehouse as if they're second-class citizens. Bruce merely visits this company value; he doesn't demonstrate it.

Timeliness is an aspect of *owning it and passionately acting on it*. For Jennifer, part of honoring that value means keeping her commitment to share her marketing update by 4 p.m. each Thursday so that important decisions can be made before the end of the week. Jennifer does that once or twice, but on the third Thursday she doesn't submit her update until Friday morning, because something came up. Eventually, her late updates become a habit. Like Bruce, Jennifer has shown that she merely visits this company value when it is convenient—she doesn't live it. These two people adopt our values when the values suit them, but the values are not embedded in their behavior. They don't consistently walk the talk. Unless values are lived and demonstrated in people's work ethic every day, they have no meaning.

As I stressed in Part One, values are an important ingredient in the "Don't Mark My Paper, Help Me Get an A" performance review philosophy. Let me reiterate that what we ideally want at WD-40 Company are high performers who are also good citizens— people who operate according to our values.

BUILDING A TRIBAL CULTURE

As I stated earlier, I asked our people to think of us as a "tribe" rather than a "team" to open their minds to the "Don't Mark My Paper, Help Me Get an A" philosophy and to open up communication in general.

> *To understand how a tribal culture impacts open communication, think about tribal leaders: They sit around a fire and share their knowledge with younger tribe members.*

That's the number-one responsibility of the WD-40 tribe—to share knowledge and encourage ongoing learning. In other words, we need to make learning inclusive and evolutionary. To create a learning culture, open communication is a must. I love what C. Northcotte Parkinson said about communication:

> "The void created by the failure to communicate is soon filled with poison, drivel, and misrepresentation."

To open up communication, I identified eight other aspects of tribal thinking that I thought were important to integrate into the WD-40 culture.

First, tribes have an *identity*. People in a tribe feel a sense of *belonging* to a group for a greater good. One of the most important desires that people have in life is a desire to belong to something. People join tennis clubs and poker clubs to feel a sense of belonging and affinity. I wanted to apply that same concept to WD-40 Company by building a culture that people actually want to belong to.

Second, tribes have *folklore* or traditional beliefs, myths, tales, and practices. Folklore in nontribal language is "We've always done it that way," which has a confrontational feel. In a tribe, folklore can be positive and enabling, or restrictive and negative. If it's restrictive and negative, we can identify it and ceremonially bury it. The whole point of folklore is to give WD-40 tribe members a way to dialogue and socialize instead of being confrontational. Now during meetings our people identify our core practices or beliefs, and they have a fruitful framework in which to discuss whether to alter traditions or leave them alone.

Third, tribes have *warriors* who are brave and determined to defend each other and the tribe as well as help each other accomplish any agreed-upon goals. At Southwest Airlines, one of the core values is having a warrior spirit—a feeling that people in their company will do whatever it takes to accomplish their goals and serve their customers at the highest level possible. That's what we expect at WD-40 Company.

Fourth, members of tribes also have *individual work*. This not only builds personal esteem and a high degree of confidence in the tribe member's own ability, but it also contributes to the well-being of the entire tribe. Then everyone can make a difference. Why? Because they do *meaningful work*. One of the important things we have done in our tribe is to come up with a definition of meaningful work:

- It is conducted in a manner that is "good and proper" in all aspects.

- It positively affects our tribe and our communities, giving our work an impact that extends beyond ourselves.

- It provides learning and growth, offers challenges, requires creativity, pushes us to surpass limits, and creates exciting results.

- It provides recognition and rewards for our achievements.

- It allows us to succeed as a team while excelling as individuals.

- It allows us to enjoy the ride, bringing humor and fun into our work.

- It fuels passion!

Fifth, tribes have *ceremony*, which in an organization translates into recognition and awards as well as orientation or integration ceremonies for new members. We want to catch people doing things right as well as make sure they are on board with our vision and values.

Sixth, tribes are *constantly evolving*. This means that the tribe doesn't want to stagnate—they want to make sure they're not settled next to a lake or pond that dries up.

> *If our lake is drying up—a product's sales are going south because of new technology or innovative competitive products—our roles as tribe members are to make sure we're moving on to another pond.*

Constant evolution is a metaphor for making sure that our organization stays adaptive and works toward the future.

Seventh, tribal customs are all about *norms* and established ways of doing things. Since we are a global company, we have to be aware of the different norms in different countries where we might be operating. Sometimes we have to use different strokes for different folks.

Finally, tribes have a unique *culture*, or tradition, dress codes, and a unique language. Again, this is an important element for a global company. Creating a learning environment and establishing a clear vision and set of values are core aspects of our tribal culture.

I got excited when I realized that the tribal concept was consistent with Abraham Maslow's hierarchy of needs.[2] According to Maslow, human needs are hierarchical and arrange themselves into five tiers: physiological, safety (security), social (affiliation), esteem (recognition), and self-actualization.

Physiological needs are at the base of the hierarchy because they tend to be dominant until they are somewhat satisfied. These are the basic human needs to sustain life itself—air, water, food, clothing, shelter, and sleep—all elements that people can attain when they have a good job. After physiological needs are met, safety/security needs become predominant. In the world of work, this means having a sense of security about your job and confidence that you will not be treated in an arbitrary way. Most organization structures naturally take care of the first and second needs—but that's where they stop.

Developing a tribal culture focuses real energy on the last three higher needs. Once physiological and safety needs are well satisfied, social or affiliation needs emerge as dominant. This is where the tribal concept really comes alive, because:

> *People are social beings and have a need*
> *to belong and be accepted by people*
> *who are important to them.*

After individuals begin to satisfy their need to belong, they want esteem—both self-esteem and recognition from others. They want to be an important member of their group. In a tribal culture, members are constantly cheering each other on and recognizing each other's accomplishments.

As soon as esteem needs begin to be adequately satisfied, self-actualization needs become important. Self-actualization is the need to maximize one's potential, whatever it may be. As Maslow expressed, "What a man can be, he must be." Thus, self-actualization is a desire to become what one is capable of becoming. This is central to the whole "Don't Mark My Paper, Help Me Get an A" philosophy.

When I first thought of the tribe model, I described it to people wherever I went, and they seemed to quickly embrace the idea. They started saying, "We're members of the WD-40 tribe."

As CEO, I continue to spread the tribe idea in every way possible. I personally visit our people around the world, including Canada, the United Kingdom, Australia, Europe, and Asia. The fact that WD-40 is now sold in more than 160 nations around the world translates into a lot of time for me in other countries. I look at one of my key roles as fostering corporate well-being, so I am frequently in the field with the tribe members to be a part of their world. I listen to them and let them know I'm there for them. I send weekly e-mails to tribe members that have a personal, quirky feel to them. In the e-mails I recognize tribe members from all over the world and include personal messages, celebrations, and concerns.

SERVANT LEADERSHIP WITH AN EDGE

To help everyone in WD-40 Company share our "Don't Mark My Paper, Help Me Get an A" philosophy and integrate it into the new culture we had created, I initiated a new leadership model dubbed "Servant Leadership with an Edge." My first exposure to servant leadership came from reading some of the work of Robert Greenleaf, who had served as director of leadership development for AT&T and later became a professor at Harvard Business School.[3] Greenleaf's philosophy was that a servant leader serves first and leads second. This philosophy was reinforced during my course work with Ken and Margie Blanchard at the University of San Diego.

As the following illustration suggests, Servant Leadership with an Edge is all about people, products, and passion. It illustrates the steps of "Don't Mark My Paper, Help Me Get an A" as a circular, continuous process beginning with our vision and values, then moving to planning and execution, followed by review and learning, and finally cycling back to vision.

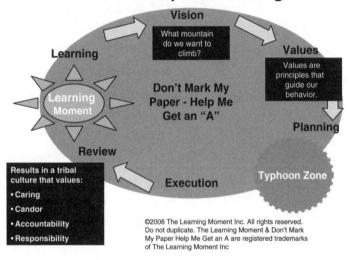

People - Products - Passion
Servant Leadership with an Edge

This total process is about creating and enabling leaders to partner for success with their people. First we define with tribe members what an A embodies, and then we create a culture where people can achieve an A. *Helping people get an A is servant leadership in action.* I hope you understand by now our desire to create an empowerment culture rather than a hierarchical, micromanaging culture. This entails *removing fear of failure* from the organization so that people can get the help they need to achieve an A.

At first look, traditional top-down "my way or the highway" managers think what we have done with our tribal culture and Servant Leadership with an Edge is too soft, warm, and fuzzy—until they track our results. Then they sit up and begin to take notice. If they bother to take a good, hard look at what we are doing (and we welcome them to do so), they soon realize that we have created a culture that is accountable—to shareholders, other tribe members, customers, and the company as a whole.

I believe WD-40 is a great company. Not only have we gotten great results, but we also have built a great place for people to work. And there's evidence to support that belief. At WD-40 Company we have our own report card on which tribe members have the option to fill out employee surveys. Every eighteen months the organization measures its performance against the agreed-upon As in terms of both company results and values. Even though the survey is voluntary, in the last round 98 percent of tribe members around the globe participated. Why is that so? I think it goes back to the tribal culture. People feel that they belong to WD-40 Company and that they're doing meaningful work. In fact, in the 2008 Employee Opinion Survey, 94 percent of tribe members said they were engaged.

TOP MANAGEMENT SUPPORT

One of my key learnings about implementing change is the importance of top management support.

If a change effort—particularly one that impacts everyone in the organization—is not central to the top managers' thinking, it probably won't succeed.

In retrospect, I think a key reason our "Don't Mark My Paper, Help Me Get an A" performance review philosophy was effectively implemented was because it grew out of my leadership point of view—my beliefs about leading and motivating people. Because the top managers' beliefs about leadership are so crucial to effecting successful change, in the next part of the book, I will share my own leadership point of view, in the hope that it will serve as a helpful example.

ENDNOTES

1. A classic reference on organizational culture can be found in Edgar Schein's *Organizational Culture and Leadership* (San Francisco: Jossey-Bass, 2004).

2. Abraham H. Maslow, *Motivation and Personality* (New York: HarperCollins College, 1987).

3. In 1964 Robert K. Greenleaf founded The Greenleaf Center, an international nonprofit organization headquartered in Westfield, Indiana. Greenleaf's 1970 essay, "The Servant as Leader," coined the phrase "servant leader" and launched the modern servant leadership movement. For more information, see www.greenleaf.org.

THREE

My Leadership Point of View

GARRY RIDGE

YOU MIGHT ASK why I want to share my own leadership point of view, so allow me to explain. In the Master of Science in Executive Leadership (MSEL) program at the University of San Diego, Ken and Margie Blanchard teach a course titled "Communicating Your Leadership Point of View." This is where I learned about the research done by Noel Tichy.[1] It shows that:

> *Effective leaders have a clear, teachable leadership point of view and are willing to share it with and teach it to others.*

Effective leaders are particularly willing to share their leadership point of view with the people with whom they work. It's my hope that this part of the book will stimulate you to think about your own leadership point of view.

My leadership point of view is best expressed by what people can expect of me, what I expect of people, and where in my background those beliefs about leading and motivating people come from. As I do that, you will see why this whole "Don't Mark My Paper, Help Me Get an A" philosophy is so core to my own thinking.

WHAT PEOPLE CAN EXPECT OF ME

My values drive what people can expect of me.[2] I have five core values, which have influenced WD-40 Company's "Don't Mark My Paper, Help Me Get an A" philosophy.

Caring

People can count on me to care about them. I want to get to know them as people, not just as tribe members working for WD-40 Company. I want to know all about their families and their joys and sorrows. I don't expect people to cut off their nerve endings at the office door.

Caring also means that I am more interested in serving people than in having them serve me. As a result, I do anything I can to help tribe members see and achieve their personal A and, in the process, realize their magnificence. If one of my tribe members is struggling to get even a B, I go out of my way to help. They should expect the "Don't Mark My Paper, Help Me Get an A" philosophy to be engraved in me.

Candor

I am candid with people, always striving to communicate honestly and openly with them. I want them to hold me accountable for my agreements, as I will hold them accountable for theirs. For example, one of my tribe members recently gave himself an A on one of his key goals, but I didn't think he was there yet. So I told him where I felt he fell short and what he needed to do to get an A in my estimation. When I worked with him on a development plan and he did get an A, he appreciated my caring candor.

Mutual Trust and Respect

I strive to create an environment of mutual trust and respect where I do what I say I'll do, and I expect others to do the same. People can expect me to treat them with dignity and fairness. I promise never to be what Ken calls a "seagull manager," who says nothing until something goes wrong and then flies in, makes a lot of noise, dumps on everybody, and then flies out. This behavior does not build mutual trust and respect. Instead, taking responsibility and doing the right thing are behaviors that build mutual trust and respect. People can expect my character—how I walk my talk—to be important to me.

Learning and Teaching

People can expect me to listen with the intent of being influenced, because I am a constant learner. People can expect me to ask more questions and question more answers, because even though I'm a teacher, I certainly don't know it all. That doesn't mean I won't share something I've learned, such as Ken's "Give Them the Final Exam at the Beginning of the Semester" philosophy. But I want any good idea—no matter where it comes from—eventually to be "our" idea.

Persistence

People can also expect me to be determined and persistent, refusing to give up and holding the belief that we all have something significant yet to do.

WHAT I EXPECT OF PEOPLE

I expect tribe members who work with me to get good results and enjoy the ride, because they are doing meaningful work that makes a difference—not only to our company, but also to our customers and each other. I expect people to have fun in the process. I want tribe members who work with me to bring their best selves to work. I love to work with passionate, motivated people who are willing and open to change and who desire to do better all the time. I expect them to have a drive to succeed and have those around them succeed, too. Tribe members who work with me need to be caring and candid with me if we are to be partners; they must tell me the truth about what I need to do more of and what I need to do less of to help them win and accomplish their A. They need to be comfortable with being accountable and holding me accountable, too. I tell people:

> *Believe in yourself. Never give up,*
> *and take one day at a time.*

I want and expect every tribe member to win. I expect confidence without arrogance—champions who are not cocky.

Where did those expectations come from? They came from my life experiences—my background.

MY BACKGROUND

I was born in Sydney, Australia, in 1956. From the beginning, my family was central in my life. In fact, I learned a great deal from all of them—Dad, Mum, and my brothers and sister—because they were all adults to me. You see, I was *really* the youngest of four children. I say "really" because when I was five years old, my nearest sibling was seventeen.

From an early age, I had an interest in people. I cared about people. This undoubtedly was stimulated by the attention I got from my brothers and sister. They took me to places and events where people fussed over me. They seemed to care about me. This gave me a feeling that I was important and made me realize that everyone needs to be special and recognized by important people in their lives.

I got my character and doing things the right way from my dad and my persistence and determination from my mum.

My dad had a tremendous work ethic. He worked for the same company for fifty years. When he retired, I was only sixteen. This meant that as I started my work life journey, Dad was available as my business mentor and coach. That became very important to me. Why? I was not a great athlete as a kid; I never really played on any sports team in school. This meant that I wasn't a big hit with the girls. So while my mates were out on the sports and social scene, my interest in learning outside the normal school system grew through my work in a variety of jobs—delivering milk, selling papers, washing cars, and working at the local dry cleaners, hardware store, or sports store.

As I got fascinated by business, enter my dad. I can still hear him say, "Garry, it's a fair day's work for a fair day's pay. You should always do your best for the people and company who hired you. You need to be reliable. You need to be sure you keep your commitments. You don't need contracts in life, Garry. You just need a heart, a handshake, and a commitment."

My mum was the real persistent driver. She gave me priceless advice that impacted the rest of my life. She told me, "You can be anything you want to be and do whatever you want to do. Just hold your head up high and never give up." I am sure my sometimes-blind determination to do and be the best comes from her. Mum is in her late nineties today and still has that determination. She is a "climb any mountain" type, whereas my dad was more the other side—"You've got to do it the right way."

What I learned from my family was augmented during my teenage years by three businessmen who cared enough to allow me to learn from them—Jack Lambert, Warren Knox, and John Eckley. They owned the sports store, hardware store, and dry cleaners in my area. I would work for them after school and during the holidays. Each gave of himself to share what he had learned over the years. They taught me vital things about business. At a young age I learned key lessons:

We're here to serve the customers. Service matters. The product we give our customers matters. Your attitude matters.

For example, Jack Lambert used to repair tennis rackets. I remember one day watching him regut and restring a racket. It took him hours to do this one racket. I said to him, "Mr. Lambert, why do you spend so much time stringing one tennis racket?" He said, "Garry, someone will play an important game with this racket. They're depending on the quality of my work for the result they get."

I remember when I worked in the hardware store, how the store looked was really important to Mr. Knox. He would say, "If you expect people to come in and shop at your store, it's got to be appealing and inviting. It's got to provide a warm and attractive atmosphere."

As for John Eckley, the owner of the dry cleaners, he treated every shirt, jacket, and pair of socks as if they were his own.

These three gentlemen gave me a playground on which to practice business. They let me do things. If I didn't pay attention, they didn't scold me; they coached me. They said, "Hey, how would it be if we tried it this way?"

I remember when Warren Knox's father died. He left me alone to take charge of the store for two days. He just turned over the keys to me and said, "You know what to do." And I did. I ran the store for him during those two days. I opened the store. I made sure the product was out. I handled the money. When he came back and I gave him his keys, he didn't question anything. He taught me how to get an A, and he knew I would be an A player when he was gone.

Many times I reflect on the tremendous influence my family and these three businessmen had on me and my success in business. Later in life, their caring mentorship motivated me not to let my work life stop me from being a good mentor for my son and daughter in the early years of their business lives—as well as others who might need some coaching.

Being around adults all the time made me comfortable interacting with and talking to a wide range of people. As a result, I have never had a problem communicating up and down the age ladder.

As I progressed through life, I became more and more curious about why things were the way they were. I remember a TV show called *Why Is It So?* A professor, Julius Sumner Miller, would ask a question and then provide the answer. I also took a real liking to the TV character Columbo, who asked a lot of questions in a simple way. He never let complexity or confusion get in the way of the obvious. This character and the professor fueled my desire to understand as well as learn.

A huge Learning Moment was moving to the United States in 1994. Coming from Australia, I was given a free pass. People would say, "He wouldn't know. He's from Australia." Soon the value of not knowing—or just being brave enough to admit I didn't know—was real to me. It was hard at first, because we all want to show how much we know, or we're embarrassed to admit we don't know. After a while, though, I got comfortable with those words, "I don't know," and developed the courage to use them.

It's amazing how much more you learn when you admit you don't know.

MY BELIEFS ABOUT LEADING AND MOTIVATING PEOPLE

My leadership point of view is driven by my determination to make a difference, do worthwhile work, get good results, and, at the same time, have fun.

Making a Difference

From the time I was a child, the desire to make a difference has been central to my being. In many ways it has driven my desire to be a leader. I want to help others make a difference.

I remember when I was a paper seller in Australia at the age of ten. I sold papers not because I needed the money. The money was hardly worth getting up at five o'clock on Sunday mornings or getting home at seven or eight o'clock each night after pushing a paper cart miles and miles. I wanted to make a difference.

The first difference I made—I can remember it quite clearly—was in delivering papers to people who depended on me for their source of news. Many of them were elderly, and I was the way they got their daily news. One of the most rewarding times was delivering the paper to Mrs. Peel, one of my older customers. Because she was in poor health, I always took her paper to the front door. She always opened the door with a smile. She showed her appreciation by giving me a big bag of lollies (candy) every Friday. Mrs. Peel showed me I made a difference.

This concept—making a difference—has followed me through my life.

If I can make a difference doing something, I become passionate about it. No difference, no passion.

Doing Worthwhile Work

Over the years I have been involved in a number of businesses and community organizations. It has become clear that doing worthwhile/meaningful work—an outgrowth of my desire to make a difference—is a driving force in my leadership point of view. This was certainly true during my involvement in community radio in Australia. I'd been involved in the activities of my local city council. Although I had been asked to run for a higher local office, I could not get passionate about it.

Then one day Peggy Womersley, the mayor of the city, approached me about another possibility. The city had invested considerable money in developing a local radio station. The station was to serve two purposes. First, it was to be a community base to broadcast radio shows for groups ranging from religious organizations to special ethnic programs. Second, it was to be a training base for communication students.

The station was well behind its plan both financially and functionally. The council was considering abandoning the project. Peggy asked me to take on the job of chairman of the board of the station, even though I had no radio experience. If I accepted the position, I had six months to raise enough funds from the community to be viable and get the station on the air.

I recognized this as an opportunity to make a difference. Although the station had debt and there was infighting within the volunteer group, I saw this as challenging, worthwhile work. The goal was clear: be on the air in six months. Within that time frame, we not only had the station on the air, but I was doing a three-hour radio program every Sunday morning—and having fun doing it. Programs were being produced and aired for six different ethnic groups, plus many other special-interest groups.

Today, seventeen years later, the station is still going strong. With great pride, I have hanging on my wall the Baulkham Hills Shire Council Outstanding Community Service Award. It's a wonderful reminder of this leadership learning experience.

Getting Good Results

It became obvious to me early in life that good results were the reward of hard, smart work.

At the age of twenty I got a job as a traveling salesman for an auto parts and accessories company in Sydney. The owner of the company, Wally Ryan, had convinced me I should leave Waltons—the retail chain where I had just completed my three-year management training course—and join his company to help develop his business.

On the day I arrived at the office, I was greeted by Wally, an aggressive Irishman, who informed me I was about to get an education on how important it was to get results. He showed me my new company car—pretty nice for a guy of twenty to have a company car—and then handed me a suitcase full of license plate frames.

In Sydney, there is a famous highway called Parramatta Road, which runs from Parramatta to the city, about twenty-five miles. Parramatta Road was famous in those times as the road of car dealers. Every good, bad, and indifferent car dealer was located on Parramatta Road. My mission was simple: start at one end of the road and work toward the city. Come back to the office on Friday and bring the orders.

Selling license plate frames to car dealers was not fun; Wally had thrown me into the deep end. He had confidence I could swim, he gave me the chance, and all I needed to do was paddle like hell. Determined not to let him down, I worked twelve hours a day selling my way up Parramatta Road.

At the end of the week, when I brought back my orders, I had outsold all the other salespeople.

Having Fun

When you're passionate about something, working on it is fun. I love Ken's view of passion.

A passionate activity is one you're doing without regard for time.

When you do what you love, you lose track of time. To that I would add: and having fun doing it!

Having fun to me is seeing people develop along the path to our shared vision. I get some of my biggest rewards when I see people excel, especially those with whom I've had the opportunity to share experience and learning. Having fun is helping others understand what they want to become and then helping them achieve their dream—which is not necessarily the dream I might have for them.

Having fun is the reward of a true servant leader—one who leads with love and is not afraid to encourage trust, respect, and confidence.

FINAL THOUGHTS

My dream is to have WD-40 Company viewed as a leadership laboratory for business, where ideas such as the tribal culture and the "Don't Mark My Paper, Help Me Get an A" philosophy can be formulated, tested, and tweaked. Our ultimate mission and goal, of course, is to create shareholder value. But as part of that process, we are using this learning laboratory to develop great leaders who can go out into the world to make it a better place for all.

Does your company reach the WD-40 gold standard? To get a "good on ya," here are the questions you should answer for your organization. Our tribe members call it "Garry's Top 10 + 1." If you can answer all of these in the affirmative, give me a call—we're mates!

1. Do you have a clear, meaningful, and easily understood vision/mission?

2. Do you have the right people in the right seats on the bus?

3. Do you have a meaningful BHAG (big hairy audacious goal), and have you communicated it to your people?

4. Are your values driving the behavior you want in the organization?

5. Are you creating a culture that increases employee engagement?

6. Are you cultivating a spirit of internal and external learning?

7. Do your people know what an A looks like, and are you supporting them to get that A?

8. Are your products/services creating lasting, positive memories for your customers?

9. Do you have the best, most timely data and information to help your organization make good business decisions?

10. Are your key performance indicators the right ones, and are you measuring what matters?

11. Do you celebrate success?

ENDNOTES

1. Noel Tichy, *The Leadership Engine: How Winning Companies Build Leaders at Every Level* (New York: Harper Collins, 1997).

2. I learned from Drea Zigarmi and Susan Fowler at the University of San Diego that a value is something that I hold dear, a lasting belief that a particular end or means is more personally acceptable than another, something that is chosen freely from among alternatives with an understanding of the outcome, and something that must be publicly prized and acted on. Zigarmi is coauthor of *Leadership and the One Minute Manager* and *The Leader Within*. Fowler is coauthor of *Self Leadership and the One Minute Manager*.

FOUR

The Simple Truths About Helping People Win at Work

Ken Blanchard

The following twelve simple truths are just that—simple but powerful. They are all about the thinking, beliefs, and behavior that are necessary to partner for performance with people the way that Garry did at WD-40 Company. No matter where you are leading—in the office, at school, at church, at home, or in the community—the real question is

Are you going to mark people's papers, or help them get an A?

The answer Garry Ridge chose made all the difference for the people of WD-40 Company.

As you read through Part Four, you'll notice that I reference a number of my published books. That wasn't done to blow my own horn, but rather because I thought you should know where these thoughts came from.

– SIMPLE TRUTH 1 –

Performing Well: What Makes People Feel Good About Themselves

In *The One Minute Manager*,[1] Spencer Johnson and I have a saying: "People who feel good about themselves produce good results." When you think about it, there's some truth to that statement. When you feel good about yourself, you tend to work harder and try to perform the best you possibly can.

However, after *The One Minute Manager* came out and people were using that quote all the time, I thought that maybe we got caught in the old human relations trap of trying to make people feel good about themselves regardless of the results they produce.

As a result, I changed that quote when I wrote *Putting the One Minute Manager to Work*[2] with Bob Lorber. The saying became

"People who produce good results
feel good about themselves."

What I've found over the years is that it's hard to keep up good morale and human satisfaction if people are losing—if the results they're getting aren't making a difference. The relationship between results and human satisfaction has become important over the years in all the consulting and training activities that The Ken Blanchard Companies has been involved in. It's not that we focus on just getting results. As Spencer Johnson and I argued in *The One Minute Manager* and Jim Collins contended in *Good to Great*,[3] it's a both-and process:

Both people and *results are important.*

Overemphasizing either one can cause problems. But one thing is for sure: If people are not performing well, it's hard for them to be excited about themselves or the organization where they work.

Garry Ridge has certainly found that to be true at WD-40 Company. As the company's performance continues to improve, because people are given opportunities to get As, the opinion that tribe members have of themselves and WD-40 Company continues to go higher. In the 2008 employee opinion survey, 96.4 percent of the tribe members said, "I feel I am a valued member of WD-40 Company." And 96.7 percent of them said, "I would recommend WD-40 Company to my friends as a good place to work." Those are the kinds of attitudes that people have when they're performing well.

To Help People Perform Well, an Effective Performance Management System Must Be Established

An effective performance management system has three parts. The first is *performance planning*. This is where goals, objectives, and performance standards are established.

It's all about giving your people the final exam ahead of time.

The second part of an effective performance management system is *day-to-day coaching*, or what WD-40 Company calls *execution*. This is where a manager observes and monitors the performance of his or her people, praising progress and redirecting where necessary. This is all about teaching people the answers.

The final aspect of effective performance management systems is *performance evaluation*, or what WD-40 Company calls *review and learning*. This is where you sit down with people at the end of a period of time and review their performance. In many ways, this is regiving the final exam you established with them at the beginning of the process.

Which of these three aspects of an effective performance management system do you think is most time-consuming for the majority of managers? Undoubtedly, it's performance evaluation. Managers all over the world agonize over their annual performance reviews with each of their people. Why? Because they have to fill out an evaluation for each of their people and then meet with them individually to justify their (the managers') evaluation of their direct reports. As Garry shared, at WD-40 Company every tribe member fills out only one evaluation form—his or her own. When tribe leaders meet with a tribe member, they are reviewing the tribe member's assessment of his or her own performance.

Some organizations do a good job of goal setting. But what happens after goals are set? They're filed—until an obvious performance problem occurs or somebody says to a manager, "It's time for your annual performance reviews." Then everybody starts running around, bumping into each other, trying to find the goals. The "informal/formal" meetings at WD-40 Company make sure that doesn't happen. The key here is having a final exam established at the beginning of the fiscal year. This is a living document that guides how tribe members and their leaders work together to help the tribe members get an A.

The least time-consuming aspect of performance management in most organizations is day-to-day coaching. Yet, as Garry Ridge has pointed out, this is key to implementing a "Don't Mark My Paper, Help Me Get an A" philosophy—and it's where most of the focus should be. This is when Situational Leadership® II comes into play, giving tribe members the appropriate direction and support as they journey toward an A. It provides the basis for day-to-day coaching.

– SIMPLE TRUTH 3 –

It All Starts with Performance Planning

The first secret of *The One Minute Manager* is One Minute Goal Setting. All good performance starts with clear goals. If people don't know what they're supposed to accomplish, how can they possibly get an A?

As Garry points out, the process begins with the essential functions: What are this person's major responsibilities? Once basic responsibilities or essential functions are established, three to five goals should be created. Garry and I both believe in the 80/20 Rule, which is sometimes called Pareto's Law. Eighty percent of the performance you want from a person will come from 20 percent of the activities that he or she can focus on. It's the 20 percent for which you want to establish goals. This does not mean that people don't engage in other functions or activities that are not covered by these goals, but those activities are not critical to that person's job performance.

Once goal areas are established, people need to know what the performance standards are.

What does good performance look like? What would be considered an A in this goal area?

As Garry pointed out, a SMART goal has to be specific. This means that the goal has to be observable and measurable so that both manager and direct report will know if an A is being achieved. If a goal can't be measured, it shouldn't be a goal, because no one will know whether it has been accomplished.

I'm often amazed when I look at companies' annual performance review forms. They typically ask managers to evaluate people's performance on things such as creativity, initiative, and promotability, but no performance standards are spelled out for those categories. Any evaluation would be purely subjective. Remember:

**If you can't measure something,
you can't manage it.**

A category such as creativity could be made objective by defining specifically what good performance looks like. For example, a person could be consistently high in creativity if he makes at least one suggestion every week to his supervisor about how performance could be improved. If fifty-two suggested improvements a year sounds like too many, the manager and direct report could lower that number and establish how many suggestions would equal an A in creativity. Remember, a SMART goal has to be attainable. If it's too easy, it won't motivate anybody. If it's too hard and a person feels there is little chance of accomplishing the goal, discouragement will set in. It's interesting that on the 2008 WD-40 Company Employee Opinion Survey, 94.6 percent of WD-40 employees indicated: "I am encouraged to offer ideas and suggestions for new and better ways of doing things."

Clear goals have to do with expectations. That's one of the things that WD-40 Company does well. On that same employee opinion survey, 97.5 percent indicated "I know what results are expected of me," and 96.8 percent confirmed that "the work assigned to me is challenging and interesting."

In *The One Minute Manager* Spencer Johnson and I suggested that people write each goal on a single piece of paper and that it take no more than a minute to read. The key here is that the goal should be written down and available for both manager and direct report to track on a daily basis. Goals that are filed away—only to be reviewed at the end of the year—are worthless. They certainly don't do that at WD-40 Company.

– SIMPLE TRUTH 4 –

The Biggest Impact on Performance Comes from Day-to-Day Coaching

While goal-setting provides direction and gets performance started, as I have suggested, what keeps performance going and helps achieve the goals is day-to-day coaching. Unfortunately, this is the step in the performance management system that is missing in most organizations. Particularly after goals are set, they are filed. Managers go to an abdicating style until annual performance review time or a problem develops. As we've pointed out, when a performance problem develops during the year, these leaders become seagull managers—they fly in, make a lot of noise, dump on everybody, and fly out. This is not very motivating for people, nor is it helpful in encouraging good performance.

Once goals are set, managers should stay in constant communication with their people so that both parties know how things are going and can stay on top of what's required to get an A. That's why Situational Leadership® II is used throughout WD-40 Company as one of the key concepts driving their day-to-day coaching process.

While Garry talked about Situational Leadership® II in his remarks, let me put the appropriate meat on the bone. Situational Leadership® II is based on two beliefs:

- People can and want to develop.

- There is no best leadership style to encourage that development.

Managers should tailor their leadership styles to the situation.

To become effective in using Situational Leadership® II, managers need to master three skills: *diagnosis*, *flexibility*, and ***Partnering for Performance***. None of these skills is particularly difficult, but as Garry and the folks at WD-40 Company have found, they require commitment from top management, practice, and reinforcement.

When it comes to diagnosis, people go through four developmental levels as they move from dependence to independence in doing a task. Each of these development levels is a combination of competence (knowledge and task-relevant experience) and commitment (motivation and confidence). The four developmental levels are as follows:

- The *Enthusiastic Beginner* (D1: low competence, high commitment) is excited but has little knowledge or experience.

- The *Disillusioned Learner* (D2: low to some competence, low commitment) finds that learning the task is tougher than he or she thought it would be, so discouragement has set in.

- The *Capable But Cautious Performer* (D3: moderate to high competence, variable commitment) knows how to do the task but lacks the confidence to do it on his or her own.

- The *Self-Reliant Achiever* (D4: high competence, high commitment) is confident and motivated and has the necessary skills to complete the task without much supervision.

Before beginning any diagnosis, goals and performance standards have to be set if Situational Leadership® II is to be effective. At WD-40 Company, since leaders and their tribe members partner for performance throughout the process, these aspects of the final exam are done together at the beginning of the fiscal year.

Once the final exam is established for a direct report, the planning process continues. The leader and direct report examine each goal to determine direct report's development level. It's important not to pigeonhole people into any particular development level. In reality, development level applies not to a person, but to a person's competence for and commitment to doing *a specific goal or task*. In other words, an individual is not at any one development level overall.

> *Development level varies from goal to goal and task to task.*

An individual can be at one level of development on one goal or task and be at a different level of development on another goal or task. For example, a person in your marketing department could be exceptional when it comes to rolling out new products and opening new markets. In this aspect of her job, she is clearly a Self-Reliant Achiever (D4). However, when it comes to hiring talent and developing people, she is very inexperienced because she has never done it before on her own. Depending on her motivation for the task, she could be either an Enthusiastic Beginner (D1) or a Disillusioned Learner (D2).

When I was a college professor, I loved to teach and write. Those were tasks I performed well and without much supervision. However, when it came to administrative matters such as managing my budget and filling out reports, I was a Disillusioned Learner at best. As these two examples show, sometimes it takes not only different strokes for different folks, but also often different strokes for the same folks on different aspects of their jobs.

What does "different strokes" mean for the leader? That person needs to master the second skill of a situational leader: *flexibility*—being comfortable using a variety of leadership styles.

The Situational Leadership® II Model

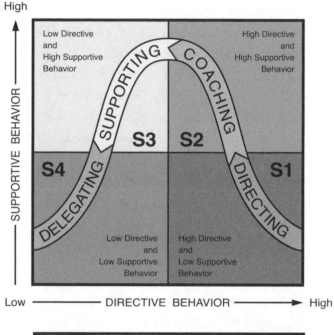

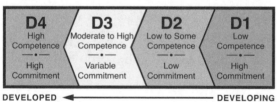

Development Level of the Individual

As shown in the Situational Leadership® II Model diagram, four basic leadership styles—*directing* (S1), *coaching* (S2), *supporting* (S3), and *delegating* (S4)— correspond with the four development levels. Each of the four styles is a combination of two leader behaviors: directive behavior and supportive behavior. The best way to describe the difference between these two leader behaviors is to go back to my days in education. At the time there were two approaches to teaching. One we called the "empty barrel" philosophy of teaching. The assumption was that the students came to class with an empty barrel of knowledge and experience on the subject being taught. So the teacher's job was to fill the barrel. Directive behavior is a barrel-filling style.

The other form of teaching was called the "full barrel" philosophy. The assumption was that the students came to class with their barrels full of knowledge and experience, but maybe it wasn't well organized for the subject being taught. As a result, the teacher's job was to draw out the students' knowledge and experience and help them apply it to this classroom experience. Supportive behavior is a barrel-drawing-out style.

Suppose you hire four new salespeople. Although three responsibilities are required of an effective salesperson besides selling (service, administration, and team contribution), let's focus on just the sales part of the job.

One of your new hires is fresh out of college and is clearly an Enthusiastic Beginner (D1). He's never sold anything, but you think he has real potential to be a top salesperson because of his personality and commitment to learning. You clearly need a "barrel-filling" directing style (S1). You have to teach your new hire everything about the sales process, from making a sales call to closing a sale. If you know about a good basic sales program, you might even want to start there.

You take him on sales calls with you so that you can show him how the sales process works and what a good job looks like. Then, you lay out a step-by-step plan for his development as a salesperson. In other words, you not only pass out the final exam, but you also are involved in teaching him the answers. You provide specific direction and closely supervise his sales performance, planning and prioritizing what has to be accomplished for him to get an A. Teaching him and showing him what experienced salespeople do—and letting him practice in low-risk sales situations—is the appropriate approach for this Enthusiastic Beginner.

Suppose another of your new hires has some sales training and experience, but he had a bad experience in his first sales job. He had a hands-off sales manager who let him go out on his own and then seagulled in when he wasn't performing well. He understands the basics of selling but is finding it harder to master than he thought. He likes your willingness to gamble on him, even though he is a bit discouraged about whether he has what it takes to become a successful salesperson. This salesperson is a Disillusioned Learner.

What's needed now is a barrel-filling and barrel-drawing-out *coaching* (S2) leadership style, which is high on both direction and support. You continue to direct and closely monitor his sales efforts, but you now engage in more two-way conversations, going back and forth between your advice and his questions and suggestions. You also provide a lot of praise and support at this stage, because you want to build his confidence, restore his commitment, and encourage initiative. While you consider your salesperson's input, you are the one who makes the final decisions, since he is learning on actual clients.

The third salesperson you have hired has a fair amount of experience in the field. She knows the day-to-day responsibilities of selling and has acquired some good sales skills. Yet she has some self-doubt and questions about whether she can sell well on her own, without your help or the support of her colleagues. You believe she's competent and knows what she's doing, but she's not so sure. She has a good grasp of the sales process and is working well with clients, but she's hesitant to be out there on her own. She may become self-critical or even reluctant to trust her own instincts. At this stage, she is a Capable But Cautious Performer (D3), whose commitment to selling fluctuates from excitement to insecurity.

This is when a barrel drawing out/*supporting* (S3) leadership style is called for. Since your direct report has learned her selling skills well, she needs little direction but lots of support from you to encourage her wavering confidence. Now is the time to stand behind her efforts, listen to her concerns and suggestions, and be there to support her interactions not only with clients but also with others on your staff. You encourage and praise, but rarely do you direct her efforts. The supporting style is more collaborative; feedback is now a give-and-take process between the two of you. You help her reach her own sales solutions by asking questions that expand her thinking and encourage risk-taking.

The fourth new salesperson you hire hits the ground running and becomes a key player on your team right away. In his previous sales positions, not only did he master sales tasks and skills, but he also took on challenging clients and was successful with them. He anticipates problems, listens carefully to clients' concerns, and is ready with workable solutions. He is justifiably confident because of his past success in managing his own sales area. Not only can he work on his own, but he also can inspire others.

This salesperson is obviously a Self-Reliant Achiever (D4) in the sales part of his job. You can count on him to hit his sales goals. For a person at this level of development, a delegating leadership style (S4) is appropriate. He can fill his own barrel when necessary and draw out any information that is needed to achieve his goals. Your job now is to empower him by allowing and trusting him to act independently. What you need to do is acknowledge his excellent performance and provide the appropriate resources he needs to carry out his sales duties. It's important at this stage to challenge your high-performing salesperson to continue increasing his sales ability and cheer him on to even higher levels of sales.

As you can see from these examples, leaders need to give their people what the people can't give to themselves.

Situational Leadership® II is helpful to tribe leaders and members at WD-40 Company at the beginning of the fiscal year, when they are determining what leadership style a tribe member needs to accomplish an A. It also is extremely useful during the quarterly informal/formal conversations.

To me, the curve in the leadership styles portion of the Situational Leadership® II model is like a railroad track. Each of the four leadership styles depicts a station along the performance curve. If you start with an Enthusiastic Beginner (D1) using a directing style (S1), and you eventually want to get to delegating (S4), which is appropriate for a Self-Reliant Achiever (D4), what two stations do you have to stop at along the way? Coaching (S2) and supporting (S3).

You'll notice that no railroad tracks go directly from directing (S1) to delegating (S4). What happens to a fast-moving train if it goes off the tracks? It gets derailed, and people get hurt. It's important for managers not to skip a station as they manage people's journey to high performance. By staying on track and stopping at all the stations, you help your direct reports to perform well on their own, with little or no supervision.

The railroad track also works the same way in reverse. If you're delegating to a supposed Self-Reliant Achiever, and a problem occurs, rather than going straight back to a directing style (S1), you go to a supporting style (S3) to find out what's gone wrong. Then, together with your direct report, you can decide whether you should go back to a delegating style (S4), because that person is now ready to run on his or her own again. However, if that person not only lacks confidence, but also needs a refresher at the skill level, you might have to go back to a coaching style (S2).

At WD-40 Company, as part of the quarterly informal/ formal discussions, tribe leader and member together examine each agreed-upon goal area and the performance progress. If a tribe leader has been using a directing style (S1) and the tribe member is progressing, that leader might want to agree to less supervision. If a tribe leader is using a coaching style (S2) and the tribe member is continuing to grow, a movement to a supporting style (S3) with periodic lunch meetings might be appropriate. The same goes for moving from a supporting style (S3) to a delegating (S4) style.

If a tribe member's performance is not progressing in a given goal area, tribe leader and member might agree to move backward through the railroad track.

The key is communication. Communication allows progress to be praised (movement forward through the railroad track) or efforts to be redirected (back through the railroad track) if necessary. As you've learned, the key to feedback at WD-40 Company is caring and candor. To be effective, feedback has to be an ongoing process. It's all about teaching people the answers to the final exam so that they'll get an A on their performance evaluation. If someone's performance is going in the right direction, he or she needs an "Atta boy" or "Atta girl." Garry calls these "Good on ya, mates." However, if the person is coming up with a wrong answer, he or she needs to be told in a caring way, "That's a wrong answer." Then quickly ask, "What would be a better answer?"

Coaching is the "secret sauce" that makes the "Don't Mark My Paper, Help Me Get an A" philosophy a success, which is why we've spent so much time discussing it. If coaching isn't central in the process, people are left to succeed or fail on their own. Their performance review is held over them as a demotivating threat. When tribe leaders and members partner for performance, the review becomes an energizing process.

– SIMPLE TRUTH 5 –

Trust Is Key to Effective Coaching

A few years ago colleague Jim Ballard and I coauthored a book called *Whale Done! The Power of Positive Relationships*[4] with Thad Lacinak and Chuck Tompkins, who have been training killer whales at SeaWorld in Orlando, Florida, for over thirty years. Why did I get involved in writing that book? I was tired of hearing people tell me that the way they knew they were doing a good job at work was that nobody had yelled at them lately. In other words, no news was good news. I figured maybe people needed a more dramatic example to illustrate the power of building positive relationships.

It doesn't take much to convince people that it probably wouldn't be a good idea to punish a killer whale and then tell the trainers to get in the water with it. They call them "killer whales" for a reason. Working as a team, these whales have been known to take on great white sharks.

Have you ever seen a Shamu show at one of the SeaWorld facilities? Let me tell you, there is no negative interaction between the trainers and the whales. What was most interesting to me was hearing that when they get a new whale—whether from another facility or a newborn—they don't do any training with that whale for weeks. All they do is feed and play with it.

When I asked why SeaWorld had this extended no-training period, they said, "We want to convince the whale that we mean it no harm." What a wonderful concept!

The problem in most organizations is that there is little trust between managers and their direct reports, because managers often have to sort their people into normal distribution curves or, even worse, rank-order their people.

One of the most powerful results of WD-40 Company's "Don't Mark My Paper, Help Me Get an A" philosophy is that people trust their managers, because they see them as their performance partners. In fact, 94.5 percent of people on the 2008 WD-40 Company Employee Opinion Survey indicated, "I trust my supervisor." It is also interesting to note that trust moves even further up the hierarchy. When presented with the statement "I trust the global tribal council to make sound decisions in the best interests of the company," 96.5 percent of WD-40 Company employees answered "yes."

To teach people how important it is to build trust, one of our colleagues, Cindy Olmstead, developed the TrustWorks®: Leader as Trust Builder® program with Luanna Olney and Nancy Jamison.[5] They were motivated to create this program by research that suggested that leadership trust is not the "soft" issue that many in the business world generally and incorrectly perceive it to be. For example, at Stanford University a distinguished group of theorists and researchers gathered to examine the impact of trust on organizations.[6] They found that leaders who have the trust of their employees maximize productivity, creativity, and loyalty in their organizations.

When a leader does not create a climate of trust, people

- Question decisions

- Have moral problems

- Fail to participate fully

- Avoid taking creative risks, and ultimately leave the organization

When employees do these things, the organization is deeply and measurably impacted by

- Reduced quality of the product or service

- Increased cost of turnover, hiring, and training

- Missed opportunities that would have been captured by fully dedicated and creative employees

In another study, Watson Wyatt found that companies whose employees trust the top executives posted 42 percent higher shareholder returns.[7]

Olmstead, Olney, and Jamison feel strongly that building leadership trust is an economic issue directly affecting the bottom line—and so do I.

Without trust, it's difficult if not impossible to inspire commitment and loyalty from your people. Without those ingredients, you won't have passionate employees who will go out of their way to serve your customers.

– SIMPLE TRUTH 6 –

The Ultimate Coaching Tool: Accentuating the Positive

People can get four consequences as a result of their performance:

- No response

- Punishment or a negative response

- A positive response

- Redirection

Our notorious seagull managers focus on the first two consequences. They leave their people alone until something goes wrong, and then they move in quickly with a negative response. Effective managers focus on the last two: positive responses and redirection.

If someone told me, "Going forward, you can't teach anything you have been teaching over the past forty years except one thing," what I would hold onto is this:

The key to developing people is to catch them doing something right.

I am a big fan of accentuating the positive. That's the basis for One Minute Praisings, the second secret of Spencer Johnson's and my book, *The One Minute Manager*.

Once goals are clear, managers should not disappear until an annual performance review. Instead, they should constantly wander around—as managers do at WD-40 Company—to see if they can catch their people doing something right and praise them for their efforts.

It is important to remember that you should not wait until people do something perfectly right to praise them. Praise progress, because it's a moving target.

Imagine if, in teaching your children to walk, you stood them up and said, "Walk!" Then, when they fell down, you spanked them and shouted, "I told you to walk!" What would be the result? Probably you'd have eighteen-year-old kids crawling around the house. So you don't do that. We all intuitively understand that when children fall, we praise them for standing. When they eventually take their first steps before falling, we praise that progress. This goes on until eventually they gain their balance and start to take some real steps.

At WD-40 Company ongoing feedback and praising progress are a way of life. Why? Because they don't leave it to chance. Peter Drucker often said, "Nothing good ever happens by accident." To get the results you want, some structure is needed to provide the necessary support and accountability. At WD-40 Company, daily use of Situational Leadership® II and quarterly informal/formal discussions provide the structure to encourage feedback and praise. Does it work? Yes. In the 2008 WD-40 Company Employee Opinion Survey, 90.5 percent of the workforce indicated, "My supervisor gives me good ongoing feedback regarding my performance."

It's important to note that this process is not a one-way street of only supervisors giving feedback to their people. Since everyone fills out their own progress report, they are also expected to evaluate their own performance and catch themselves doing something right. The job of the tribe leader is to review the tribe member's self-evaluation. Then together they can celebrate any progress. Managers and their tribe members are a team in making sure that people have a good chance to get an A.

– SIMPLE TRUTH 7 –

Redirection Helps Get Performance Back on Track

In *The One Minute Manager*, Spencer Johnson and I talked about redirection in the section on One Minute Reprimands. We differentiated reprimands from redirection by asking whether the person whose performance was being observed was a learner on a particular task or an experienced achiever. Reprimands are for "won't do" attitude problems, while redirection is for "can't do" skill problems.

If I were asked to redo any part of *The One Minute Manager*, I would emphasize redirection more than reprimands. Why? Because of new technology, today things are moving so fast that just when a person becomes competent in doing something, that job changes. People are continually asked to become learners. In fact, if you are not an ongoing learner today, your career may be in jeopardy. Consequently, managers are expected more and more to be teachers and coaches; therefore, the need for redirection is much more prevalent than the need for reprimands.

As I discussed in Simple Truth 5, "Trust Is Key to Effective Coaching," no negative interaction occurs between the killer whales and trainers at SeaWorld. Again, you don't want to punish a killer whale and then ask trainers to get in the water with it. So what do they do when a killer whale doesn't perform a trick up to standards? When the whale comes back to the stage, the trainer doesn't reward it with a bucket full of fish. What the trainer does is give the whale a hand signal that says either "Let me see that again" or "Why don't you do a trick you know well?"

The purpose of redirection is to set up, as soon as possible, an opportunity for praising to occur.

What makes an effective redirection? First, just as with praising, redirection must be given as soon as possible. For example, suppose you require each of your direct reports to give you a sales report every Friday afternoon. Before you go home one Friday, you notice that your new hire didn't comply with that requirement. Rather than waiting until Monday, you go to that person and tell her, "You didn't get your sales report in this afternoon." Giving prompt feedback is important.

The second thing that makes redirection work is explaining specifically what went wrong, as well as the impact it is having on team performance. Using the preceding example, you could say, "When I don't get reports from all our team members, I can't do a complete analysis for my Monday leadership meeting."

The third part of an effective redirection, if appropriate, is for the manager to take responsibility. For example, you might say, "Maybe I didn't make it clear enough that I expected a sales report from you by 1 p.m. every Friday."

The fourth part of an effective redirection is to reiterate the importance of the task. You could say, "Tracking our sales on a weekly basis is important. Not only do I need it for my Monday leadership meeting, but also tracking our sales helps us celebrate our progress or redirect our efforts if need be. That way we have no surprises at the end of the year."

Finally, an effective redirection reassures the person you still have confidence in him or her. You could say, "I'm still excited about having you on our team, and I know you'll be a good team member."

At WD-40 Company, redirection, in many ways, is an outgrowth of a Learning Moment. It helps a potential winner to keep moving toward an A. Consistent with the WD-40 philosophy, this responsibility rests not just with the manager, but also with the tribe member. As Garry says, "It's a partnership. Both sides are responsible." They're accountable to each other: "We owe each other for something we agreed on."

– SIMPLE TRUTH 8 –

Deliver Reprimands with Caring Candor

Is reprimanding someone ever appropriate? Absolutely.

While the reprimand can be construed as a negative consequence, if it is delivered with caring candor in the WD-40 style—which is the way Spencer Johnson and I intended—it can be a powerful motivator for high performers whose recent goal achievement, for some reason, is not up to its normal high standards.

An effective One Minute Reprimand has four steps.

First, it should be delivered in a timely manner—as soon as the unusual poor performance is detected. A reprimand should never be saved for an annual performance review.

Second, it should be specific. Using the example we gave for redirection in the preceding Simple Truth, you might say, "You didn't turn in your weekly report on time."

Third, the manager should share his or her feelings about the performance—frustration, disappointment, surprise, or the like. "I'm upset about your not getting your weekly report in on time. It's frustrating to me, because it prevented me from doing a complete analysis of our team's performance."

Finally, a reprimand should end with a reaffirmation of the person's past performance. "The reason I'm upset is because this is so unlike you. You're one of my best people, and you usually get your reports in on time."

> *The reason this step is important is that when you finish giving someone a reprimand, you want him thinking about what he did wrong, not how you treated him.*

This final step—the reaffirmation—is often missed. After giving negative feedback, many leaders storm away. I'll never forget giving my then-teenage son Scott feedback about parking his humongous truck (if you put guns on it, you could go to war) in our driveway, blocking my wife, Margie, from getting out and me from getting in. When he arrived home in a friend's car, I raced out of the house, told him immediately what he'd done wrong in very specific terms, and then shared with him my angry feelings. When I turned to go back into the house, Scott jumped out of his friend's car and followed me all the way into the kitchen and said, "Dad, you didn't give me the last part of the reprimand. You love me. I'm a good kid. This is so unlike me." All I could do was laugh and acknowledge that he was right.

A reprimand should be used only when you are talking to a normally strong performer. If you are giving feedback to someone who is inexperienced but a potential winner, you cannot reaffirm that person's past efforts, because he or she is still learning. With those people, redirection is more appropriate.

Again, with the WD-40 partnership philosophy, people might beat their supervisor to the punch and reprimand themselves at one of the quarterly informal/ formal discussions or even sooner, if appropriate. The important thing is to not let the performance of a high achiever gradually go downhill.

– SIMPLE TRUTH 9 –

Performance Reviews Should Be About Retaking the Final Exam

In many organizations, the annual performance review is a mystery to most of the people being reviewed. They might have set goals at the beginning of the year, but usually those goals are filed away and seldom revisited. At the end of the year, people wonder how they will be evaluated. In some ways, so do their managers, who now spend hours preparing performance reviews for each of their people.

I ask people all the time if they have ever received any surprises during their annual performance review—feedback that was news to them. They laugh, because it happens all the time.

With the "Don't Mark My Paper, Help Me Get an A" philosophy, this would never happen. Why? Because, as Garry explained, everyone completes only one performance review—their own.

The performance review *is* essentially a review. Of what? You can bet it's a review of the feedback they received during their four informal/formal discussions, or any time along the way. There are literally no surprises here, because all discussions focus on the final exam that they agreed on at the beginning of the year, or modified at one of the quarterly informal/formal discussions.

The job of tribe leaders is to fill out their own performance reviews, to be reviewed with their tribe leaders. When it comes to their tribe members, they sit down individually with each one and review each member's self-assessment. If anyone disagrees with a review, tribe leader and tribe member go back to the agreed-upon essential functions and performance indicators from the final exam they agreed on at the beginning of the year to determine why the disagreement has occurred.

"Not everyone gets an A," Garry says, "but that is the aim." If someone receives a B, that person plays a major role in that evaluation. Now together manager and tribe member determine what has to be done and what help is needed to get that A next time. This takes any fear out of a performance review, because both manager and team member are accountable and responsible.

If, after a period of time, it becomes clear to both tribe leader and tribe member that an A is not possible— that person is perpetually a learner or has been stuck for a long time as a C performer, even with the right help—the focus switches to career planning, because the person might be in the wrong job. If this is a values-driven tribe member, a different opportunity in WD-40 Company will be explored. If this isn't a values-driven tribe member, as Garry explains, "We will share them with a competitor." Maybe that person can get an A in another organization.

– SIMPLE TRUTH 10 –

Developing and Sharing Your Leadership Point of View Is a Powerful Communication Tool for Your People

One of the reasons Garry's "Don't Mark My Paper, Help Me Get an A" philosophy was successfully implemented at WD-40 Company was that it was consistent with his leadership point of view. Why is that important? Because research has shown that one of the key requirements for any successful change effort is top management support.

Do most leaders know their leadership point of view? According to Noel Tichy,[8] effective leaders have a clear, teachable leadership point of view and are willing to share it with and teach it to others—particularly the people with whom they work. This realization so impacted me that, as Garry mentioned, my wife Margie and I created a course called "Communicating Your Leadership Point of View" as part of the Master of Science in Executive Leadership (MSEL) program at the University of San Diego.[9]

I believe that effective leadership is a journey, beginning with self-leadership, moving to one-on-one leadership, and then team leadership, and ending with organizational leadership. This course is the final focus of the self-leadership portion of the degree program. The course culminates in all the students making presentations to the class that describe their leadership points of view. The students deliver their leadership points of view as though they are talking to those who report to them in their organizational leadership positions. Garry went through that very process. Clarifying his leadership point of view motivated him to develop the WD-40 Company "Don't Mark My Paper, Help Me Get an A" philosophy.

If you as a leader can teach people your leadership point of view, they may also begin to solidify their own thinking about leadership so that they can teach others, too. Tichy feels strongly that learning, teaching, and leading are intricately intertwined and, therefore, should be considered inherent parts of everyone's leadership description. Why everyone's? Because:

Everyone is a leader in some part of their job or their life. Whenever you attempt to influence someone else's beliefs, thinking, or behavior, you're engaging in leadership.

So think about your own leadership point of view. What can people expect from you, and what do you expect from them? Once you are clear on these expectations, ask yourself questions such as these: Where did those beliefs come from? Who were the leadership role models in the early part of my life? Do I have a life purpose and a set of operating values? What guides my leader behavior?

Once you can answer these questions, you can share the answers with your people. When you share your leadership point of view with your people, not only will they have the benefit of understanding what they can expect from you and what you expect from them, but they also will know where that thinking came from. It also puts pressure on you to walk your talk, since you have made public your leadership point of view.

That's exactly what Garry has done with the people at WD-40 Company. Implementing a "Don't Mark My Paper, Help Me Get an A" philosophy provided the structure for him to walk his talk.

- SIMPLE TRUTH 11 -

Servant Leadership Is the Only Way to Go

As you learned in Part Two, "Building the Right Culture," the integrating framework for the WD-40 Company "Don't Mark My Paper, Help Me Get an A" philosophy was dubbed "Servant Leadership with an Edge." As Garry mentioned, Robert Greenleaf coined the term "servant leadership" in 1970 and published widely on the concept for the next twenty years. Two thousand years ago, servant leadership was central to the philosophy of Jesus, who exemplified the fully committed and effective servant leader. Mahatma Gandhi; Dr. Martin Luther King, Jr.; and Nelson Mandela are more recent examples of leaders who have exemplified this philosophy.

Yet servant leadership is an odd concept. When I talk about it, people often raise their eyebrows. They think it means the inmates are running the prison or that it's about pleasing everybody. These people don't understand what servant leadership is all about, the way Garry Ridge does. Two aspects of servant leadership are practiced in the "Don't Mark My Paper, Help Me Get an A" philosophy—vision/direction and implementation.

VISION AND DIRECTION

Vision and direction is the leadership part of servant leadership. In establishing a compelling vision, the traditional pyramidal hierarchy is alive and well. This doesn't mean that top managers don't involve others in crafting the vision, but the responsibility for vision and direction lies with them. Everyone looks to the president, their department chairman, or their supervisor to understand, in Garry's terms, "what mountain they want to climb." As Garry says, "A clear vision must be more than a business case. No one wants to get an A in a class they don't believe in."

A number of years ago I asked Jesse Stoner to write a book with me titled *Full Steam Ahead!*[10] Jesse had been studying the power of vision for both individuals and organizations for more than twenty years. She determined that a compelling vision—one that engages the hearts and minds of others—has three parts:

- *Your purpose.* What business are you in? Where are you going, and why?

- *Your picture of the future.* What will your future look like if you are accomplishing your purpose?

- *Your values.* What do you stand for? On what principles will you make your ongoing decisions?

**A compelling vision tells people who they are,
where they are going, and what will
guide their journey.**

Walt Disney started his theme parks with a clear purpose. He said, "We're in the happiness business." That is very different from being in the theme park business. Clear purpose drives everything the cast members (employees) do with their guests (customers). Being in the happiness business helps cast members understand their primary role in the company.

At WD-40 Company everyone is clear that they are in the "squeak, smell, and dirt" business. Their products take care of squeaks and get rid of smells and dirt. As Garry puts it, "What could be clearer than that?"

If your organization does not have a purpose statement, if your purpose statement is not worded so that everyone understands it, or if people are not excited about your purpose statement, your organization will begin to lose its way.

Walt Disney's picture of the future was expressed in the charge he gave every cast member: "Keep the same smile on people's faces when they leave the park as when they entered." Disney didn't care whether guests were in the park two hours or ten hours. He just wanted to keep them smiling. After all, they were in the happiness business. Your picture should focus on the end result, not on the process of getting there.

At WD-40 Company their picture of the future is that if they do a good job at the squeak, smell, and dirt business, it will create positive, lasting memories for their users.

The view of the future is what keeps people going when times are tough. It prevents your organization from stopping short or arriving at the wrong destination.

Values are the nonnegotiable principles that define character in an organization. My observation is that fewer than 10 percent of the organizations around the world have clear, written values.

Values are important, because they drive the behavior of the people who are working on your purpose and your picture of the future.

Most companies that have stated values do not have them rank-ordered. Why is that important? Because, as Garry indicated, life is about value conflicts. When these conflicts arise, people need to know which value they should focus on.

The Disney theme parks have four rank-ordered values: safety, courtesy, the show, and efficiency. Why is safety the highest-ranked value? Walt Disney knew that if guests were carried out of one of his parks on a stretcher, they would not have the same smiles on their faces leaving the park as they had when they entered.

Here are the rank-ordered values that guide tribe member behavior at WD-40 Company:

1. Doing the right thing
2. Creating positive, lasting memories in all our relationships
3. Making it better than it is today
4. Succeeding as a team while excelling as individuals
5. Owning it and passionately acting on it
6. Sustaining the WD-40 economy

So at WD-40 Company, no matter what's happening, *doing the right thing* is the first order of business.

Once you are clear in your organization about who you are (your purpose), where you are going (your picture of the future), and what will guide your journey (your values), you can set meaningful goals. Why do I say that? Because a compelling vision provides a context for your goals. It makes your goals come alive and makes them relevant.

IMPLEMENTATION

The servant part of leadership—implementation—signals the need to philosophically turn the pyramidal hierarchy upside down.

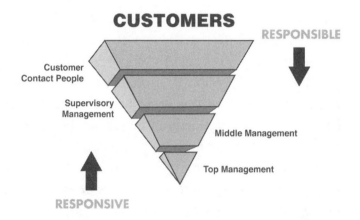

The Implementation Role of Leadership

Here the frontline people can be responsible—able to respond to their customers with a sense of autonomy. In this scenario, leaders serve and are responsive to people's needs, training and developing them to soar like eagles so that they can accomplish established goals and live according to their vision and values.

Organizations run by self-serving, egotistical leaders never risk what Garry Ridge has done at WD-40 Company. By philosophically turning the traditional pyramidal hierarchy upside down, he's made it a major responsibility of every manager to help their people get an A. In organizations run by self-serving leaders, the traditional hierarchy is kept alive and well. People throughout the organization are often judged and sorted into arbitrary performance categories. This not only eliminates trust, it also demotivates people. Rather than taking responsibility for making things happen, people protect themselves by bowing to the hierarchy. When something goes wrong, they act like ducks and say, "It's our policy. Quack, quack. I just work here. Quack, quack. I didn't make the rules. Quack, quack. Do you want to talk to my supervisor? Quack, quack." This is dramatically different from the eagles you will find at WD-40 Company, who are soaring above the crowd and taking care of business.

Vision and direction get things started with leadership, but it's the servant aspect that really makes things happen.

To discover whether that statement is true, Drea Zigarmi and Scott Blanchard worked with Vicki Essary to study the interaction between organizational *vitality* and success, employee *passion* and success, customer *devotion* and loyalty, and leadership. In their year-long study,[11] which included an exhaustive literature review of hundreds of studies from 1980 to 2005, they examined two kinds of leadership: strategic and operational. Strategic leadership focuses on vision and direction (the leadership aspect of servant leadership), while operational leadership focuses on implementation (the servant aspect of servant leadership).

Interestingly, Zigarmi and Blanchard found that while strategic leadership is a critical building block for setting the tone and direction, it has only an indirect impact on organizational vitality. The real key to organizational vitality is operational leadership. If this aspect of leadership is done effectively, employee passion and customer devotion will result from the positive experiences and overall satisfaction people have with the organization.

It is also interesting to note that positive employee passion creates positive customer devotion. At the same time, when customers are excited about and devoted to the company, this has a positive effect on the work environment and the employees' passion. People love to work for a company where customers are raving fans. It makes them gung ho, and together the customers and employees directly impact organizational vitality.

The big-picture conclusion from the research of Zigarmi and Blanchard is that the leadership part of servant leadership (strategic leadership) is important, because vision and direction get things going. But the real action is with the servant aspect of servant leadership (operational leadership). When leaders with vision serve their people by helping them achieve their goals and treating them with respect and dignity, that kindness is returned to their customers—who in turn keep the business thriving.

– SIMPLE TRUTH 12 –

Celebrate Successes

When we were writing *The Power of Ethical Management*,[12] I asked Norman Vincent Peale why the press didn't report more good news. He said, "I'm so glad they don't! If good news were news, there wouldn't be much of it going on. The only reason bad news is news, is because there's not much of it happening." What a wonderful perspective! When I watch the news, I hear mostly tragic stories, but then I realize that millions of people got home safely that night, took care of their families, and did good things. It's just that nobody says much about them.

The same is true with organizations. In general, and in business in particular, it's assumed that we don't need to celebrate the good news.

When you find good stories in your organization, celebrate them!

I think one of the greatest things in the world is the free enterprise system. Whether it's in this country or others, there's nothing more heartening than to see people taking the opportunity to build a business that not only serves customers well but also creates opportunities for people in the organization to win and soar like eagles. And there are some really outstanding examples. Yet you wouldn't know that from reading the newspaper or listening to TV news. Most of what's reported about business is negative. As a result, the impression the general public gets is that all businesses are bad and that they're run by self-serving, egotistical leaders who are only concerned about themselves.

That's why I'm excited about this series of books spotlighting leaders and companies who are successfully practicing an aspect of *Leading at a Higher Level*. It's been a joy to do this first book in the series, featuring Garry Ridge and the successes at WD-40 Company. As I travel around the world, I find a number of people discouraged about how they are managed and evaluated. They feel judged, sorted out, and rank-ordered. They don't really feel that their managers are on their side, because the managers are under the gun to find a few winners and identify a certain number of losers.

I've talked about the "Don't Mark My Paper, Help Me Get an A" philosophy all over the planet. From Europe to Australia to China, people's eyes light up when I tell them that it's the responsibility of a manager to help people get an A. They're amazed when I explain that if a manager doesn't do anything to help a person perform well, that manager could get fired, not the poor performer.

WD-40 Company is such a great story. As a company it not only has tremendous performance by Wall Street standards and every other financial measure, but it also has a high level of human satisfaction. It's a win/win story.

So celebrate the good stories in your organization! Let other people know about them. Let those stories be good role models so that people can say, "Look what they're doing in that department. Maybe we should be doing that in our department."

I encourage you to find good stories not only in your own organization, but also in other organizations in your community. Publicize them so that people can learn about and perhaps replicate them, or even improve on them. The point is:

Celebrate successes!

ENDNOTES

1. Ken Blanchard and Spencer Johnson, *The One Minute Manager* (New York: William Morrow, 1982, 2003).

2. Ken Blanchard and Robert Lorber, *Putting the One Minute Manager to Work* (New York: William Morrow, 1984).

3. Jim Collins, *Good to Great: Why Some Companies Make the Leap and Others Don't* (New York: Collins Business, 2001).

4. Ken Blanchard, Jim Ballard, Thad Lacinak, and Chuck Tompkins, *Whale Done! The Power of Positive Relationships* (New York: Simon & Schuster, 2002).

5. More information on this program is available at www.blanchardlearning.com.

6. Roderick Kramer and Tom Tyler, eds., *Trust in Organizations: Frontiers in Theory and Research* (Thousand Oaks, CA: Sage Publications, 1995).

7. Watson Wyatt 2007/2008 Communication ROI Study, "Secrets of Top Performers: How Companies with Highly Effective Employee Communication Differentiate Themselves" (Arlington, VA: Watson Wyatt, 2008). For more information, see www.watsonwyatt.com.

8. Noel Tichy, *The Leadership Engine: How Winning Companies Build Leaders at Every Level* (New York: Harper Collins, 1997).

9. For more information on this program, visit www.sandiego.edu/business/programs/graduate/leadership/executive_leadership.

10. Ken Blanchard and Jesse Stoner, *Full Steam Ahead! Unleash the Power of Vision in Your Company and Your Life* (San Francisco: Berrett-Koehler, 2003).

11. Scott Blanchard, Drea Zigarmi, and Vicky Essary, "Leadership-Profit Chain," *Perspectives* (Escondido, CA: The Ken Blanchard Companies, 2006).

12. Ken Blanchard and Norman Vincent Peale, *The Power of Ethical Management* (New York: William Morrow, 1988).

Epilogue

Ken Blanchard and Garry Ridge

IT WAS INTERESTING for us to discover that our fathers had a similar philosophy. It can be summed up by the statement "Talk is a lot of hot air unless you back it up with some action." In other words, don't say what you'll do; do what you say. Or as Gandhi said, "Be the change you wish to see in the world." This book could be a lot of hot air unless it stimulates you to do something. If you've been complaining about how your performance is evaluated, share this book up the hierarchy. If you're a top manager and you've been hearing some rumblings about how performance is evaluated in your organization, you might want to look in the mirror.

One of our favorite stories is about the guy who opens his lunch at work and complains, "Baloney sandwich! That's the fifth day in a row I've had a baloney sandwich. And I don't even like baloney."

One of his coworkers, trying to be helpful, suggests, "Why don't you tell your wife to make you some other kind of sandwich?"

"My wife—forget about it!" said the complainer. "I make my own sandwiches!"

Is your performance review system full of baloney? If so, what role have you played in creating it? In what ways are you responsible for what's not working?

Not all managers are like WD-40 Company tribe leaders. Many still believe you need to use a normal distribution curve that grades a few people high, a few people low, and the rest average. The reason these managers and their organizations are often reluctant to discard the normal distribution curve is that they don't know how they will deal with career planning if some people don't get sorted out at a lower level. If they rated a high percentage of their people as top performers, they wonder how they could possibly reward them all. As people move up the hierarchy, aren't there fewer opportunities for promotion?

We believe that question is naïve. If you treat people well and help them win in their present position, as they do at WD-40 Company, they often will use their creativity to come up with new business ideas that will expand your vision and grow the organization. Protecting the hierarchy doesn't do your people or your organization any good.

Ralph Stayer, coauthor with Jim Belasco of *Flight of the Buffalo*,[1] tells a wonderful story that proves this point. Stayer was in the sausage manufacturing business. His secretary came to him one day with a great idea. She suggested they start a catalog business, because at the time they were direct-selling their sausages to only grocery stores and other distributors. He said, "What a great idea! Why don't you organize a business plan and run it?" Soon the woman who was his former secretary was running a multimillion-dollar new division of his company and creating all kinds of job opportunities, as well as revenue for the company.

Leadership that emphasizes judgment, criticism, and evaluation is a thing of the past. Leading at a higher level today is about treating people the right way by providing the direction, support, and encouragement they need to be their best. If you help your people get As, your performance management system will ignite them to blow away your customers with outstanding service. Why? Because people who feel good about themselves want to return the favor.

ENDNOTE

1. Jim Belasco and Ralph Stayer, *Flight of the Buffalo: Soaring to Excellence, Learning to Let Employees Lead* (New York: Warner Books, 1994).

A
The WD-40 Company Goal
Review Form

Definitions of ratings: A or A+ defines success. L is an acceptable standard of performance. B is an opportunity to be better through an action plan. C is unacceptable results, requiring an improvement plan to be in place, and it impacts bonus eligibility.

A+	A+ = I consistently deliver EXCEPTIONAL performance and behavior, and my results indicate that I have achieved my A+ "stretch" goals. • I can pass the "public opinion test," meaning that my reputation, exceptional contributions, and performance results are well known by others. • My first and second coaches are proud to hold up both my job performance *and* conduct as the standard that all other tribe members should strive to achieve. • I consistently go above and beyond to demonstrate each corporate value, and I teach others how to demonstrate corporate values. • I exhibit a high skill level, am a role model/mentor to others, am self-directed, and demonstrate good morale that positively affects others. • I have contributed on a single or several occasion(s) in an exceptional, significant nature, of great value to the company.
A	A = My results indicate that I have ACHIEVED my goal through performance and behavior. • I substantially meet all expectations of job description and goals, and I function independently in my coach's absence. • I diligently apply myself in meeting expectations. • I perform all the critical aspects of the position as expected. • Process improvement: I create successful new processes. • I assist others in meeting their objectives. • I demonstrate the corporate values.

B	B = I have an opportunity to be BETTER. I am on the path to an A, but there is room to do better. • I am making the effort needed and am improving toward meeting expectations. • I do not meet all the critical aspects of the job expectations, goals, and/or results. • An action plan is in effect to get me to an A, including learning and leadership involvement. • I demonstrate most of the corporate values.
L	L = I am in LEARNING mode. It is a new position for me, or I am new to the company and need more time to gain competence. • I do not meet all the critical aspects of the job expectations and/or goals, but I am progressing to an acceptable level of competence. • In the absence of my coach, I cannot function independently. • An action plan is in effect to get me to an A, including learning and leadership involvement. • I attempt to demonstrate corporate values, but I am not yet fully competent.
C	C = Lack of effort. • Does not meet critical aspects of the position and needs to apply oneself more consistently to meet expectations and/or goals. • An improvement plan is in effect, and my effort is necessary to meet expectations. • Little attempt to demonstrate corporate values; visits some corporate values.

Tribe Member's Name:	Coach Name:
Tribe Member's Title:	Review Period: Fiscal Year 2009 (9/1/2008–8/31/2009)
Essential Functions: What's an A and A+	Results
1.	
2.	
3.	
4.	
5.	
Overall Rating—Essential Functions:	

	Rating				
	Q1	Q2	Q3	Q4	FY
	Rating: A+, A, B, L, C				

Goals/Initiatives: What's an A and A+	Results
1.	
2.	
3.	
4.	
5.	
Overall Rating—Goals/Initiatives:	

	Rating: A+, A, B, L, C				

Tribe Member's Name:	
Corporate Values	Behavioral Results
We value doing the right thing.	
We value creating positive, lasting memories in all of our relationships.	
We value making it better than it is today.	
We value succeeding as a team while excelling as individuals.	
We value owning it and passionately acting on it.	
We value sustaining the WD-40 economy.	

Note: Three "Visits" in a single grading period = overall rating goes down 1 grade for that period. **Overall Rating—Corporate Values:**

Overall Quarterly Rating:

	Demonstrates or Visits				
	Rating: D, V				
	Q1	Q2	Q3	Q4	FY

Strengths	Learning Opportunities
Comments from Coach	Comments from Tribe Member
Coach Signature / Date	Second Coach Signature / Date
Human Resources Signature / Date	Tribe Member's Signature / Date

Learning Initiatives for Next Fiscal Year:		
Other:		
Signed Code of Business Conduct		Y / N
Overall Rating:		Increase %:
Current Pay: $ Hour / Year		
New Pay: $ Hour / Year		

About the Authors

Ken Blanchard has had an extraordinary impact on the day-to-day management of millions of people and companies. He is the author of several best-selling books, including the blockbuster international bestseller *The One Minute Manager*® and the giant business best-sellers *Leadership and the One Minute Manager, Raving Fans,* and *Gung Ho!* His books have combined sales of more than 18 million copies in more than twenty-five languages. In 2005 Ken was inducted into Amazon's Hall of Fame as one of the top twenty-five best-selling authors of all time. The College of Business at Grand Canyon University bears his name.

Ken is the chief spiritual officer of The Ken Blanchard Companies, an international management training and consulting firm. He is also coauthor of *Lead Like Jesus* and cofounder of Lead Like Jesus, a nonprofit organization dedicated to inspiring and equipping people to lead like Jesus.

Garry Ridge is president and chief executive officer of WD-40 Company, headquartered in San Diego, California. WD-40 Company is the maker of the ever-popular WD-40, as well as 3-IN-ONE Oil; Solvol and Lava heavy-duty hand cleaners; and X-14, Carpet Fresh, Spot Shot, 1001, and 2000 Flushes household cleaning products.

Garry has been with WD-40 since 1987 in various management positions, including executive vice president and chief operating officer and vice president of international. He has worked directly with WD-40 in 50 countries.

A native of Australia, Garry has served as national vice president of the Australian Marketing Institute and the Australian Automotive Aftermarket Association. He received his master of science degree in executive leadership from the University of San Diego in June 2001.

Garry is an adjunct professor at the University of San Diego. He teaches leadership development, talent management, and succession planning in the Master of Science in Executive Leadership program.

In March 2003 Garry was awarded Director of the Year for Enhancement of Economic Value by the Corporate Directors forum. In April 2004 he received the Arthur E. Hughes Career Achievement Award from the University of San Diego. In 2006 Garry was awarded the Ernst & Young Master Entrepreneur Award.

SERVICES AVAILABLE

The Ken Blanchard Companies® is a global leader in workplace learning, productivity, performance, and leadership effectiveness that is best known for its Situational Leadership® II program—the most widely taught leadership model in the world. Because of its ability to help people excel as self-leaders and as leaders of others, SLII® is embraced by Fortune 500 companies as well as mid-to small-size businesses, governments, and educational and non-profit organizations.

Blanchard® programs, which are based on the evidence that people are the key to accomplishing strategic objectives and driving business results, develop excellence in leadership, teams, customer loyalty, change management and performance improvement. The company's continual research points to best practices for workplace improvement, while its world-class trainers and coaches drive organizational and behavioral change at all levels and help people make the shift from learning to doing.

Leadership experts from The Ken Blanchard Companies are available for workshops, consulting, as well as keynote addresses on organizational development, workplace performance, and business trends.

Global Headquarters
The Ken Blanchard Companies
125 State Place
Escondido CA 92029
www.kenblanchard.com
1.800.728.6000 from the U.S.
+1.760.489.5005 from anywhere

KEYNOTE SPEAKERS

Blanchard Keynote Speakers present enduring leadership insights to all types of management-related events including corporate gatherings and celebrations, association conferences, sales meetings, industry conferences, and executive retreats. Our network of speaking professionals is among the best in the world at engaging audiences to new levels of commitment and enthusiasm. **Blanchard speaker topics include:**

- Coaching
- Customer Loyalty
- Employee Engagement
- Leadership
- Motivation and Inspiration
- Organizational Change
- Public Sector Leadership
- Team Building
- Women in Leadership

To book Ken Blanchard, Garry Ridge, or another Blanchard keynote speaker for your next event, please call:

United States: 800 728-6052

United Kingdom: +44 1483 456300

Canada: 800 665-5023

International: 760 489-5005

Or visit **www.kenblanchard.com/speakers** to learn more and to book your speaker today.

SOCIAL NETWORKING

Visit Blanchard on YouTube

Watch thought leaders from The Ken Blanchard Companies in action. Link and subscribe to Blanchard's channel and you'll receive updates as new videos are posted.

Join the Blanchard Fan Club on Facebook

Be part of our inner circle and link to Ken Blanchard at Facebook. Meet other fans of Ken and his books. Access videos, photos, and get invited to special events.

Join Conversations with Ken Blanchard

Blanchard's blog, HowWeLead.org, was created to inspire positive change. It is a public service site devoted to leadership topics that connect us all. This site is nonpartisan and secular, and does not solicit or accept donations. It is a social network, where you will meet people who care deeply about responsible leadership. And it's a place where Ken Blanchard would like to hear your opinion.

Tools for Change

Visit kenblanchard.com and click on "Tools for Change" to learn about workshops, coaching services, and leadership programs that can help your organization create lasting behavior changes that have a measurable impact.

HELPING PEOPLE WIN AT WORK
WITH SITUATIONAL LEADERSHIP® II

Situational Leadership® II (SLII®) is the most widely taught leadership model in the world. SLII® provides leaders with a diagnostic approach for creating open communication and developing self-reliance in those they manage. It is designed to increase the frequency and quality of conversations about performance and development. As a result, competence is developed, commitment is gained, and talented individuals are retained.

SLII® is recognized as both a business language and a framework for employee development because it works across cultural, linguistic, and geographical barriers. The foundation lies in teaching leaders to diagnose the needs of an individual or a team and then use the appropriate leadership style to respond to the needs of the person and the situation.

Based on 30 years of research and corporate adoption, SLII® is proven to help develop leaders who excel at goal setting, coaching, performance evaluation, active listening, and proactive problem solving. By creating the systems needed to track performance and partnering, it has allowed users to clarify individual goals and ensure alignment with the organization's goals. In addition, SLII® has helped companies increase the retention of "star" employees, improve individual and organizational development, and improve job satisfaction and morale at all levels.

Contact The Ken Blanchard Companies at +1.760.489.5005 to find out how your company can develop competence, gain commitment, and retain talent.

Index

.